God of Fortune

Damrong Pinkoon

Most people
would rather run away than
face challenges in their lives.

Whether these
challenges are severe or not,
some people find a way to escape
and stay away from them.

What they don't realize is
that their challenges
don't simply go away.

They can be avoided
only for a while.

They will come back eventually.

GOD *of* FORTUNE

Out of the million on the journey, only one person will find success in life

DAMRONG PINKOON

JAICO PUBLISHING HOUSE

Ahmedabad Bangalore Bhopal Bhubaneswar Chennai
Delhi Hyderabad Kolkata Lucknow Mumbai

Published by Jaico Publishing House
A-2 Jash Chambers, 7-A Sir Phirozshah Mehta Road
Fort, Mumbai - 400 001
jaicopub@jaicobooks.com
www.jaicobooks.com

Published in arrangement with
Damrong Pinkoon Company Limited
999 Gaysorn Plaza 5th Floor, Lumpini
Pathumwan, Bangkok 10330, Thailand

GOD OF FORTUNE
ISBN 978-81-8495-672-6

First Jaico Impression: 2015

Printed by
Rashmi Graphics
#3, Amrutwel CHS Ltd., C.S. #50/74
Ganesh Galli, Lalbaug, Mumbai - 400 012
E-mail: rashmigraphics84@gmail.com

Only the brave,
who confront
their troubles, survive.

A few accept their
limited capabilities. The ones
who do not inherit talents
or special abilities,
try to practice, fight
and confront as well as accept the truth.

Because the only way
to possess a strong mind is
by daring to face their challenges.

The ones who think,
speak and do well,
possess a strong mind
and good will.

People who walk the right path
will find many stone tablets.

These will tell them
about the concepts of living.

Good thoughts,
practices of virtues, ethics,
and merit can overcome
every trouble of life.

The journey to find the reality
or the truth of life
will have many obstacles.

And only one person
in a million can find
the God of Fortune.

He has a good chance of learning
the secrets of the legend of success.

TABLET 1

Most people
need the same things,
but only a few
walk the right path to achieve them.

Some people begin with
a wrong idea, which makes them
walk the wrong path in life
and lose their direction
from the beginning itself.

So, the person who starts with
an incorrect idea,
ignoring the correct working principles,
always walks the opposite way
from everybody who is right.

People who go the wrong way
will remain lost until the end.

They will never realize
they are on the wrong path,
as they wrongly believe
that they are right.

Therefore, they keep thinking
and doing the wrong things all their lives.

The God of Fortune

1

A MYTH

After the **God of the Universe** created the universe, the sun, the moon, the stars and the earth, he allowed the gods to dwell in the stars. Each of the gods ruled a star in the universe and rotated their reign as commanded by the God of the Universe.

As for earth, the God of the Universe assigned the **God of Fortune** and the **seven angels** to rule and help human beings.

Earth was created in six days. The God of the Universe created land, mountains, trees, the seas, rivers, streams, plants, rocks, air, clouds, skies, rain, storms, aquatic life, reptiles, marine creatures and land animals, including human beings.

Everything on earth lived happily together. People adapted and grew, and with every passing day, they had more passion to develop themselves until they learned how to compete with one another.

People evolved more than any other creature on earth and changed from walking on all fours to walking on two feet.

And, since humans had their hands free, they could use them for many purposes. This helped humans gain an advantage over creatures that still walked on all fours.

Creatures that have the ability to fly had to first walk on their feet, and their arms eventually became wings. Any flying creature that did not use its wings would lose the ability to fly.

The same rule applied to other creatures on earth. Any unused ability would be swallowed by time and eventually disappear.

Humans continued to compete. They used their two hands to make many things. In the beginning, they used their hands to break the branches of trees to make hunting weapons and chased animals for food with them.

Later, humans began to use rocks and other things they dug up from the ground. They extracted minerals and benefited from them. They learned how to make containers by noticing things that happened around them.

Humans noticed that after it had rained, they could mold pieces of earth into any shape. So, a few started to mold soil into different things. They used water from streams and rivers for this purpose. Then, this molded soil was laid out under the sun. Finally, humans made containers to store water, food and other things they wanted to keep for later use.

Humans used creativity to invent things. This allowed the brain, the most-used human organ, to further develop until it made humans very different from animals.

With time, the brain made humans work hard to achieve everything they needed to make their lives more comfortable.

Humans used cotton and threads from silk-worms to make clothes and other materials. They also hunted animals for meat and used their skin as clothes in winter.

Humans hunted animals on land and creatures in the rivers and seas. Even animals much larger than ourselves could now be easily killed with the help of these modern tools. This was because humans had evolved for more than a 100,000,000 years. Therefore, this had resulted in development of varied capabilities within them.

Humans invented a means of communication called **language**. Different human cultures possess diverse languages and they constantly compete with each other.

Humans conceptualized **money**. They fought and struggled to see who had the most of it. For them, money could buy everything they wanted.

Humans continued to compete. They began to use their hunting weapons to kill one another in their pursuit for more money, which they thought was more valuable than another person's life.

Humans increasingly competed to show their abilities. They invented products for sale in order to obtain more money. Eventually, many people became wealthy, while only a few actually had just enough of money.

Then, a day came when a few people had more money than they needed and were unable to spend it all within their lifetime.

In every era, people who had a lot of money were praised and called **fortunate humans** or the **one who always had the God of Fortune by their side.**

Each era has its **fortunate human** or **the one who possesses the most money in the world.**

Every 10,000 years, there is **only one fortunate human.** Therefore, humans of each era want to be that special one.

That one person could achieve his fortune, because he traveled to meet the God of Fortune, who was the legend of the universe and the earth, as the story goes.

Only a few people were able to meet and receive the ultimate force from the God of Fortune, who dwelled on the highest point of the **Lucky Mountain.**

Every human wanted to receive it. However, most of them could not reach this destination in order to do so.

Many quit along the way, as the path was filled with obstacles and difficulties. Most people walked the wrong path and were lost. But one person every 10,000 years successfully chose the right path.

Most people
face challenges in life.

But only some of them
succeed in overcoming
these challenges.

This is not because
they have a special force
that is superior to another person's.

But
it is because
they refuse to surrender.

To walk the right path, people have to journey until they reach the highest mountain, which is so high that a person at the base of it cannot see the top.

On the way to meet the God of Fortune, people have to confront many issues that are mostly the riddles of life. They have to think and follow instructions before they can successfully become **a human of the 10,000 years** legend.

People have always told the story and the legend of the **God of Fortune,** but no one knew that in the world there were also **seven angels** who watched over and helped the lucky **human of the 10,000 years.**

This is the story that occurs every 10,000 years, when only one person is able to journey and become the **World Conqueror.**

There were plenty of stories that occurred during the millions of years before people and animals came to earth. Some creatures have survived through time, while many others have become extinct.

The God of Fortune

The Seven Angels

2

The Path

In thousands of villages on earth, a legend has been told for many generations. It speaks of a time when the moon blocks out the light of the sun. This event is the best time for people to begin their journey to find the **God of Fortune.**

Whoever walked an incorrect path would not be able to find the **God of Fortune.** He would confront the **God of Misfortune** instead, who would stick to that person and bring bad luck to him throughout his life.

Every 100 years, a strange phenomenon would occur. The moon would completely block the light of the sun. The next day would be the last day of the 100-year cycle of the phenomenon, when darkness blocks all daylight.

Millions of people began to prepare for their journey. Many of them wanted to be the one the world would remember as **the one human from the 10,000-years** legend, and the world would record their success.

Plenty of people wanted to achieve their targets, although they realized that if they did not meet the God of Fortune, the God of Misfortune would come into their lives instead.

JoJo was an 18-year-old boy who shared this dream with many other people who wanted to be part of the legend of success. He also prepared to start his journey the following day, along with his friends, who he grew up with.

Around 100 boys from the village prepared to travel to meet the God of Fortune. They were all gearing up for the next day when their journey would begin.

People from JoJo's village, as well as those from the nearby villages, prepared for it. Villages all over the world had been waiting for this, the only day in a 100 years when the day would become dark.

This phenomenon would be repeated around a 100 times until the human of 10,000 years arose and was bestowed a chance to become the sole **special human.**

In the morning, boys from around the world gazed at the sky simultaneously. The sun shone directly on the heads of everyone. Then, the black outline of the moon, which was the same size as the sun, gradually moved towards it.

The bright light from the sun was slowly covered by the black shadow of the moon. Rays of sunlight decreased until complete darkness prevailed.

All of the boys then began their journeys to find the God of Fortune. They did not know where to go and each walked separate paths and in different directions. They all thought that the path they had chosen was the right one.

JoJo and his 20 friends traveled to the north. They were not entirely confident they had chosen to walk the correct path. Nevertheless, they helped one another continue their journey.

They all believed that if they followed the brightest star, the North Star, they would definitely not get lost. The only other source of light came from the moon.

Many people headed in the same direction as JoJo and his friends. More of them started walking north after the idea of the North Star spread so that they would not get lost. Those who went in other directions changed their course and walked north too. But the fact was that no one knew if the way they took was right or not.

The crowd heading north kept growing. From a group of 10, it became a 100, then a 1,000, then 10,000, a 100,000 and then 1,000,000 in merely three months.

Life must always begin with
the right ideas and actions.

People who think incorrectly
always choose the wrong path.

Some people know that
they have chosen the wrong way.
And if they turn back and
head in the right direction,
they will walk a step closer
to their goal.

As a 1,000,000 people continued to walk on their chosen route, a huge stream with a strong and rapid current appeared in front of them.

Beside the stream stood a large stone tablet. The inscription on it was read and understood by everyone.

A man noted, *"I was here last year and didn't see this huge rock. I don't understand why it is here now."*

"I guess it was placed here by the God of Fortune. As the sun is covered by the moon in this 100-year cycle, it may have caused the rock to appear. Those who follow the right direction, would see this tablet along their entire route," said a second man.

"That seems so, because the name of the God of Fortune is written at the bottom. The God wants to tell us that we are on the right path," JoJo added excitedly.

"We choose to believe you both," said the first man, accepting the idea of his fellow travelers.

Everyone proceeded one after the other to the stone tablet to read the inscription.

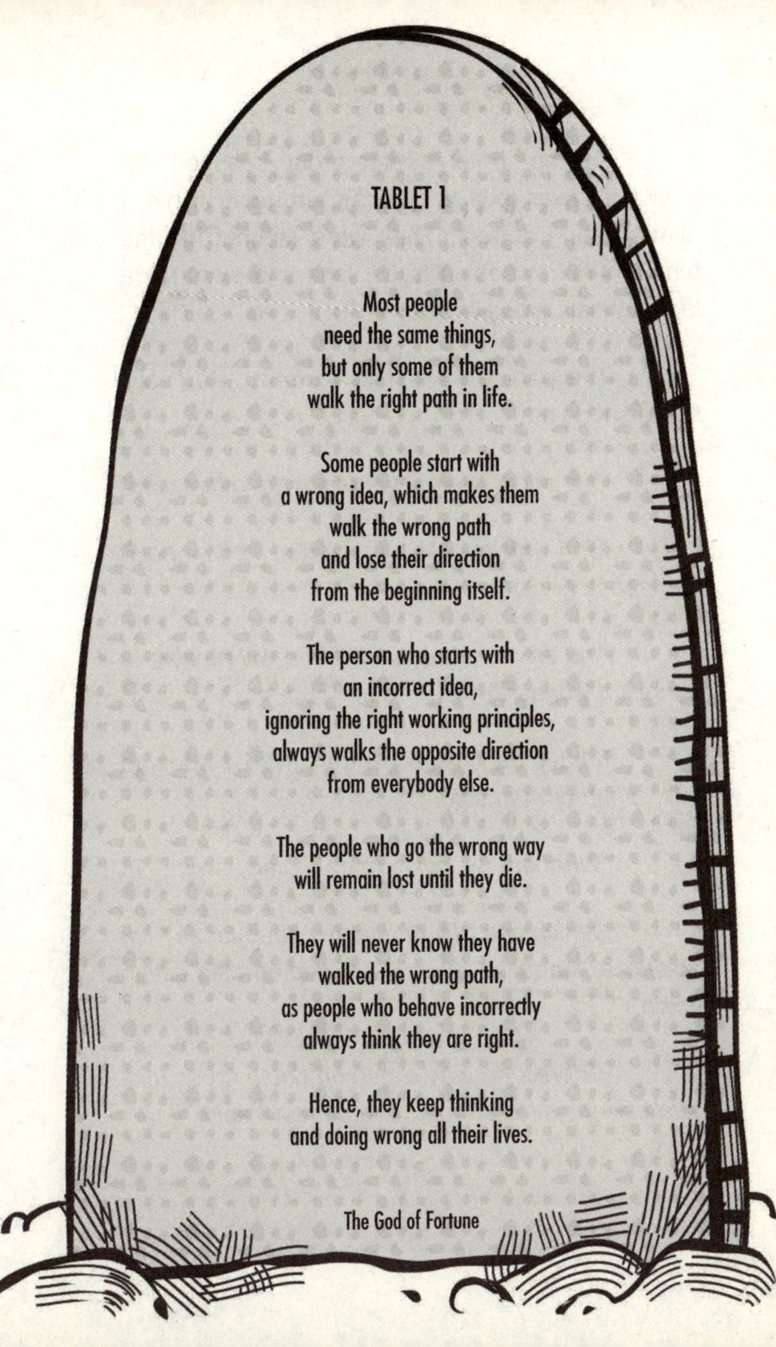

TABLET 1

Most people
need the same things,
but only some of them
walk the right path in life.

Some people start with
a wrong idea, which makes them
walk the wrong path
and lose their direction
from the beginning itself.

The person who starts with
an incorrect idea,
ignoring the right working principles,
always walks the opposite direction
from everybody else.

The people who go the wrong way
will remain lost until they die.

They will never know they have
walked the wrong path,
as people who behave incorrectly
always think they are right.

Hence, they keep thinking
and doing wrong all their lives.

The God of Fortune

As the million-strong group reached the banks of a river, they stopped and stared in disbelief at the strong current. They were stunned by the furious river, sweeping trees, logs and even large land animals along with it.

The people started to murmur and finally some spoke out.

"We will die before we reach the other side!"

"This looks like a current from hell!" someone cried out.

And then another said, "Who will be able to cross it, I wonder."

"I have my children and my wife. I won't do this," another man said.

"What are we going to do? I can't swim."

"Which one of you has any good ideas? I'm getting a headache already," a woman said sitting down.

"There's no way a person could cross this. The current is too strong," another man said.

The group stopped at the river that looked like a raging animal, flowing stronger and stronger. Dead animals floated down the river.

One of the men believed he was a good swimmer. He asked his friends to tie a rope around his waist while he attempted to swim to the other side. However, right after he jumped into the water, he was hit by a floating log and was knocked unconscious.

Days passed into weeks and weeks became months. People quickly started to run out of food. Whatever food remained was not sufficient to maintain their strength, so many of them started to gather fruits and vegetables from the land, while others caught animals to eat.

Two months later, the group that sought the famed legend was still waiting at the bank of the furious river. Many became sick and many more decided to return home, because they did not know what to do.

Many people could not wait any longer as they did not know when, or if, the water would recede. They were also unsure when the dry season would arrive. So, a lot of them decided to return to their villages.

By the third month, the group of a 1,000,000 was cut down to half. The ones who remained thought over the tough issue of what to do because only one person in 10,000 years would succeed.

If they decided not to go back to their families, they would definitely be in trouble. More importantly, if something did happen to them, no one would remain to take care of their families.

A long time later, a few people decided to continue on their quest. No matter what happened, they would overcome the obstacles. They decided to cut down trees and build ships. They used weeds to bind and fasten the timber. They built a huge mast and used their clothes to make sails which they would navigate left and right to keep with the wind.

When the first group began to work, others followed too. Many travelers divided themselves into groups and did the same thing. They all hoped to cross to the other side of the river.

People made sailboats, rafts, small boats, rowboats and anything they thought would float and support them in their efforts to cross the raging river.

They created large and small boats, even tiny rafts that could carry only two or three people.

All they could do was wait for the current to become weaker.

One morning, six months later, a man ran to the bank of the river and shouted:

"JoJo, wake up. The river seems to be calm this morning, but it won't be long. We should set sail in our large boat." It was Etto, JoJo's beloved friend, who exclaimed in delight.

JoJo and his friends hurried to the river. To their surprise, they all agreed that the river was calmer. However, they were not sure how long this calmness would last. So, everyone rushed to prepare the large boat to set sail; others also followed suit.

Ships, boats and rafts simultaneously sailed into the river in order to take their cargo to the other side. Just as most of the fleet got to the middle of the river, a strong wind suddenly picked up, scattering and damaging the small village on the bank. The ones who remained on the bank were blown away by the storm, along with their boats. This violent force of nature carried many people away.

Etto
JoJo

A few of the slowest one who had still not taken their boats to the river now were blown away by the storm. Others survived by grabbing large trees that had not been cut down to build boats.

Those who survived the initial storm let go of the trees, hoping they, too, would be blown across the river. The people in the boats looked back in horror as they saw their fellow travelers floating down the river one by one. It was such a pitiful sight.

The ones in the boats began to realize that their journey was not going to be an easy one. Everything seemed to be getting more difficult. They could not predict whether they would be able to reach the other side before the storm caught up or the strong current began again.

Meanwhile, the river began to flow stronger and the storm continued to rage and follow them. Suddenly, the smaller rafts started to lose their ability to fight the storm and the current, and eventually drifted away down the river.

The current kept gaining strength until the medium-sized boats could not endure the river's force anymore. Rowboats and rafts, too, were forced off course and away from their intended route. And, as the storm reached them, every boat that could not withstand the force of the wind and water was washed away in different directions. Only the largest ships that could deal with the force of the storm were left on the river.

It was sheer chaos and only the best-designed ships could resist the force of nature. Soon, many ships began to fall apart. People were thrown overboard, many disappeared and very few were fortunate enough to be swept along with the current to the other bank.

A large ship is like a house
with a strong structure.

When experiencing storms
or danger, a strong house
can withstand obstacles.

A small ship is like a house
with a weak structure.

When experiencing storms
or natural disasters,
a weak house cannot
withstand obstacles,
even small ones.

There were several strong boats and a few people that survived the first obstacle of crossing the river of rage.

The river, which was the first impediment, had destroyed the intention of half a million people. The number of people who remained reduced to 500,000. They had also wasted time waiting on the bank of the furious river for a few months.

Despite the rapid current and the storm, JoJo and his friends had built a ship and had successfully defeated the raging river without too much difficulty.

Theirs was the toughest ship among thousands and it survived better than the hundreds of thousands of boats and rafts that attempted the perilous crossing.

The group of people that finally made it to the other side was very glad as they learned that they had walked the right path. This was because they found a second stone tablet. The message on it read:

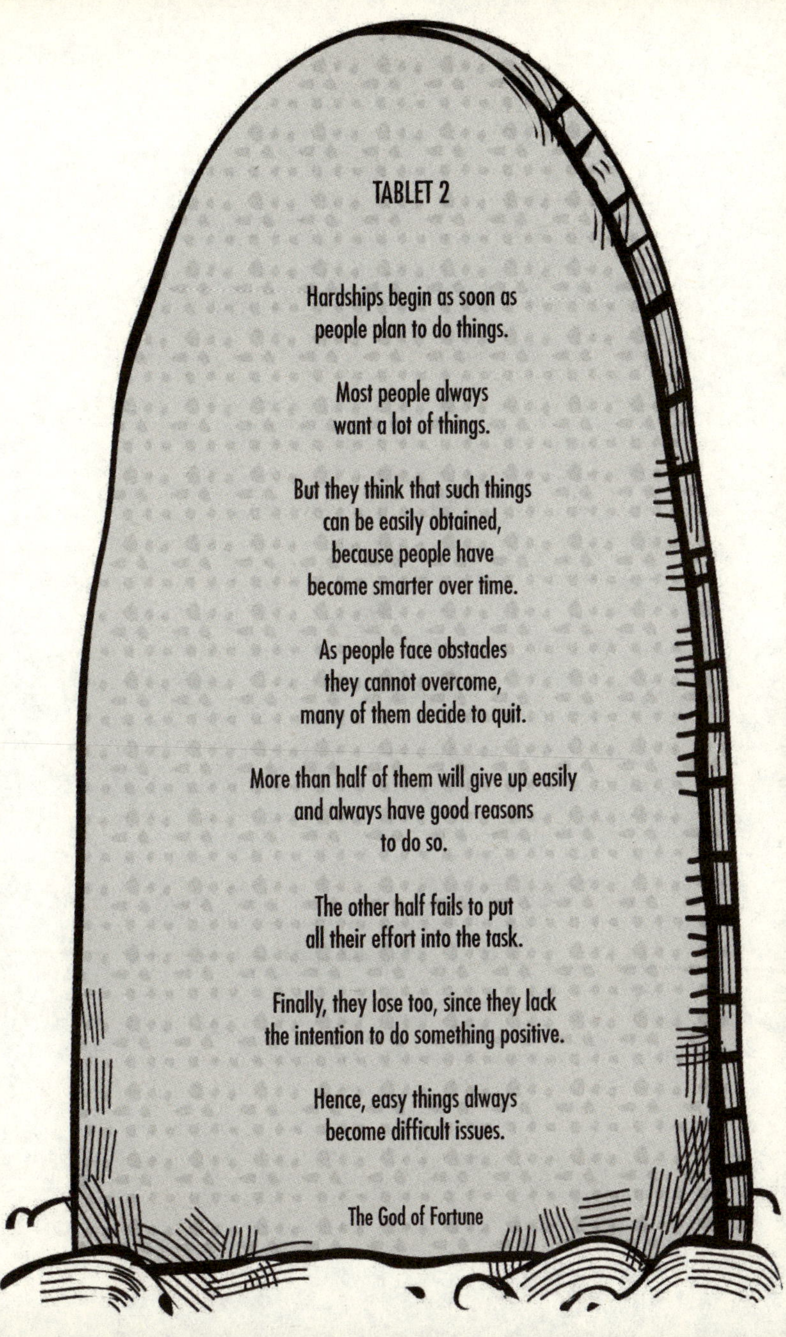
TABLET 2
Hardships begin as soon as people plan to do things.
Most people always want a lot of things.
But they think that such things can be easily obtained, because people have become smarter over time.
As people face obstacles they cannot overcome, many of them decide to quit.
More than half of them will give up easily and always have good reasons to do so.
The other half fails to put all their effort into the task.
Finally, they lose too, since they lack the intention to do something positive.
Hence, easy things always become difficult issues.
The God of Fortune

3

The Monster

A 1,000,000 people had started a journey to find what they wanted. They traveled to the north because they did not wish to get lost or just wander around without knowing their true direction and path.

Half a million people, when confronted with the first obstacle, lost their spirit. The rest crossed the river of rage, but plenty of them did not succeed.

Some of them built unstable and weak boats. When the storm broke, such boats were smashed, destroyed and sank. Some boats just vanished altogether.

From a 1,000,000 people, only a 100,000 could overcome the obstructions; they refused to surrender. These people started to exercise their abilities in thinking creatively and working harder. This enabled them to overcome their troubles.

Only one man out of ten can overcome his obstacles. Therefore, among such a huge number of people, a 100,000 out of a 1,000,000 could overcome the challenge.

The crossing of the river was just the first of a large number of obstacles and it differentiated special people from the others. Both had the same physical appearances, but it was their minds that was so different.

JoJo traveled along with the group of a 100,000 to the north. They did not lose a minute and even journeyed during the night. They did not want to rest, as they felt that they had rested enough while waiting for the storm and current to subside on the bank of the river.

JoJo and his friends continued their journey until the people at the front of the crowd cried out at the top of their voices in delight as they came across the third tablet.

Carved on the third tablet was an inscription that said:

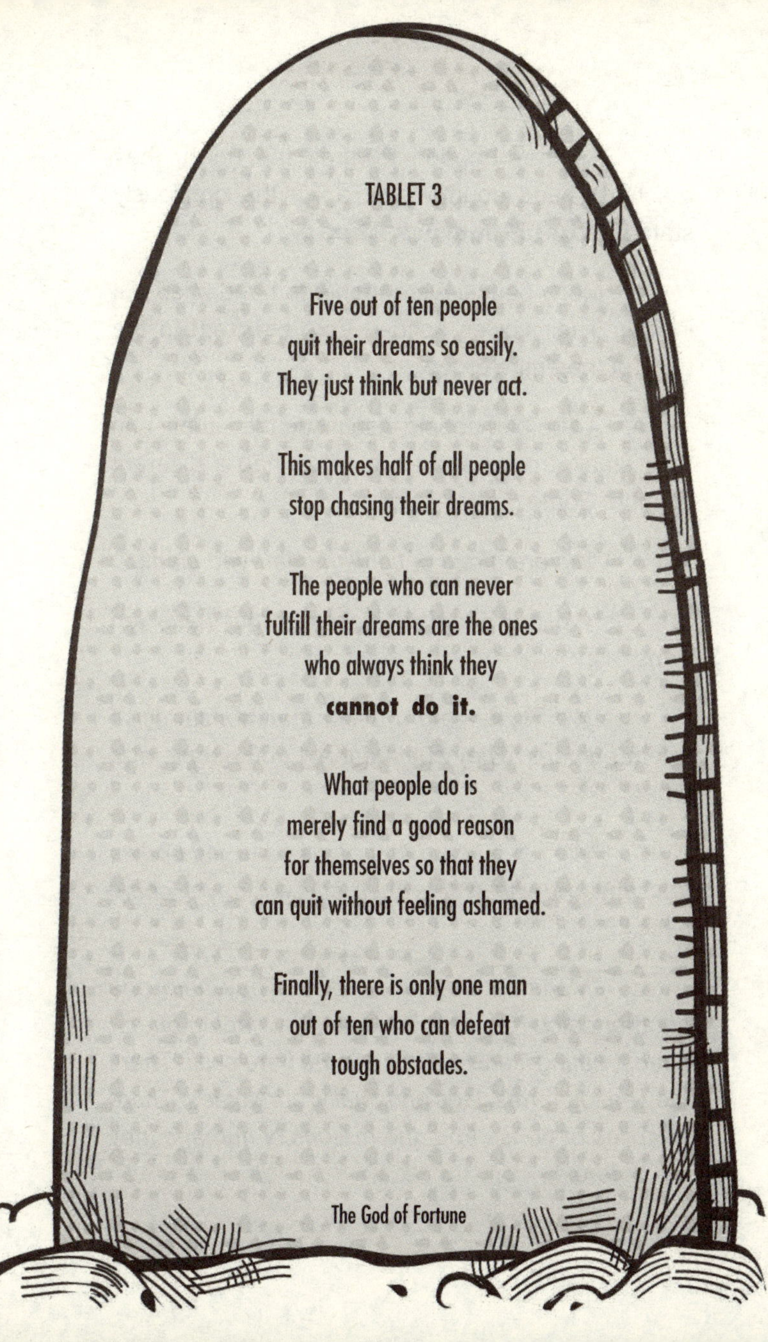
TABLET 3

Five out of ten people
quit their dreams so easily.
They just think but never act.

This makes half of all people
stop chasing their dreams.

The people who can never
fulfill their dreams are the ones
who always think they
cannot do it.

What people do is
merely find a good reason
for themselves so that they
can quit without feeling ashamed.

Finally, there is only one man
out of ten who can defeat
tough obstacles.

The God of Fortune

As they headed towards the north, they reached a huge mountain with a sign that ominously stated: **Cruel Monsters Ahead.**

Many people were frightened and cried out in fear. Their voices echoed from the front to the back of the entire group.

A 100,000 people discussed the situation in their small groups and each group had a different opinion. Some groups said:

"We are afraid of fighting one-eyed giants."

"We are afraid of monsters that have ten arms."

"We have heard a rumor that monsters like to eat humans. They could eat a 1,000 people at a time!"

"We have heard that ogres have red bodies and anyone who enters their city will never come back."

"Monsters live as families. They help one another catch humans. They start by ripping off our heads, eating it and spitting out the bare skull. Then, they eat our arms, legs and finally, our bodies. There are piles of bones from the millions of humans they ate before."

The more the group thought about the challenge ahead, the more paranoid they became. Some groups began to retreat in order to prepare themselves and get away from the enormous mountain.

Some groups decided to go back. And others hesitated as they saw more of these people retreat.

The number of people who turned their backs on the mission increased day by day. Eventually, only half of them remained. The people who returned home did so mainly because of their fear.

Most people hide
their fears within.

Sometimes they tend
to overthink
scary monsters
or
cruel creatures
or
giants,
which they do not know
and have never seen.

When something happens,
a person's subconscious
and imagination
goes into overdrive,
making us afraid
of problems.

People always have to
fight their own fears
before they fight
other things
they have never seen.

If we let
our imaginations run wild,
the results can be
unexpectedly dreadful.

The remaining people assembled together and decided to make weapons to fight the monsters. They spent a considerable amount of time creating weapons to prepare for the journey past the city of giants. Legend has it that out of the humans who entered the city, none had ever returned.

Two months passed and everyone now had a shield made from bamboo and a wooden spear with a sharp stone point. They were all fully armed and practiced various methods of throwing stones to attack a taller and larger being. They also made a large number of bows and arrows.

Although a 100,000 people had been reduced by half and now numbered only 50,000, they were equipped with weapons and were ready to fight. They arranged to meet the following morning to fight the legendary ogres.

That night, as they prepared themselves for the big fight the next morning, many of them prayed to the gods. Many people thought of their families, while others wondered how the future would be if they met the God of Fortune.

"Are you asleep, JoJo?" asked Etto, his beloved friend.

"No, can you sleep?" replied JoJo.

"I wonder what will happen in the morning. We will face the challenges of our lives," said Etto.

"Is that what you definitely think will happen?" JoJo questioned, emphasizing his friend's idea.

"Yes. Why?" Etto was curious.

"Well, your thoughts and mine are not so different. I also think that this will be the first time in my life that I will face a monster I've never seen before. But, this is the second time I've had the chance to fight side by side with my beloved friend after we crossed the river of rage together. I hope this will be a good story to tell our neighbors and a good story for our children," answered JoJo with a slight smile.

"I, too, think that our thoughts are not so different. It's just that our thoughts differ from others in the group. Most of them are beginning to feel afraid. Some are imagining that ogres have one to ten eyes, four to ten arms, and that their bodies are black or red and many other colors," Etto noted.

"But in reality, none of them has ever seen a giant. They are simply imagining it from stories that have been retold hundreds and thousands of times over the years. Those who told stories always said that they had never seen a monster with their own eyes. It's a story of the family, passed down since the time of their ancestors," Etto added.

"Now we should go to sleep so that tomorrow morning we have the strength to fight these legendary giants," JoJo said, adding good night to his friend.

"Good night," Etto replied before closing his eyes.

Beneath thousands of stars in the sky, in coldness and darkness, everybody slept in peace.

In the morning, the group prepared to fight the giants. They agreed to enter together and formed a strategic army as they had planned.

They walked past the enormous sign at the foot of the mountain. Then, they took up their formation, dividing themselves into a front troop, a left troop and a right troop.

Everyone was now a soldier who was eager to fight the legendary monsters they had been told of in various stories.

As they stood in formation, each person was heavily armed with a bow, spear, sword, stone and a short knife that they carried to the battle with the monsters.

The sound of the army's harmonious footsteps gave strength and spirit to some of the more fearful people, as the noise expressed their readiness for battle.

Some people may not be
as confident as
those who have
high self-confidence.

But for people
with a readiness
to do activities,
the fact that
they are well prepared
will help them feel more confident.

Whenever the people
surrounding someone boosts morale,
that person's courage will double.

The well-prepared army was filled with a lot of soldiers who had a well-planned strategy. It started to march forward and onward.

They walked for a considerable distance, but there was no sign of any ogre. Many people began to feel worried, as they were pretty far from the entrance, but they still found nothing.

In front of them loomed a thick blanket of fog. Its opaque color looked like clouds, which covered an enormous area. Nevertheless, the army still marched into the cloud of dense fog.

They continued walking to the sound of their footsteps, but their pace gradually became slower and slower, until none of them could hear another man's footstep. Everything fell silent. Only the sound of the wind could be heard.

Suddenly, the dense fog seemed to become so thick that none of them could see the one walking beside them.

Then, the sound of the footsteps of a gigantic object shook the ground. It seemed to be heading towards the army. Many people who were more fearful than others began to see an ogre before them, while others could see nothing at all. As they turned to look at their friends, they could not see them. It felt as though they were alone in the world.

Fear started to make some people's imaginations run wild. The images of ogres in their minds were vivid and varied.

The thick fog made everyone feel alone. Each person started to feel lonely, isolated and deserted. They felt they had no one to turn to, no company, and were totally cut off from the world.

The silence allowed the giants to appear. Some people saw an ogre with one eye, ten eyes and even a 100 eyes.

Some people saw a monster with three heads and a red body. This monster carried an axe. It was 30 times larger than any of the people whose heads did not even reach the ogre's knees.

Some saw an ogre with one eye, huge muscles and a green body. It carried an enormous hammer and was 20 times larger than any of the people. It hammered the ground every step it took towards the army, who imagined it and saw its image clearer and clearer in their minds.

The terror of the monsters in so many shapes and sizes filled each person's imagination and was created according to the stories each of them had heard during their childhood. Eventually, the image was buried deep in their subconscious, which made them see their own monster version.

People always have
a monster in their minds.

Such monsters always
have different faces.

This is because
a person's imagination varies.

When people are faced with
their ultimate fears,
their subconscious creates a cruel monster,
whose appearance differs according to
the type of hidden fear.

Therefore, the legendary ogre was a true story for everybody and was retold until it became the story of the family. All this happened because everybody hid things they feared within their minds. Such things would reappear when they felt extremely afraid, especially when they were in the land of monsters.

Some fearful people shrieked in fright. Others standing nearby heard these dreadful screams and ran away even though they could not see one another. A lot of young people turned their backs and ran to escape. They kept running as they felt a monster was chasing them.

A black monster whose weapon was an iron ball with sharp points, a blue monster who wore a strip of cloth made from the skins of a 1000 tigers and a brown ogre with a bald head and short legs carrying a two-pointed spear chased them; so did a pink giant with sharp teeth and a multiple-eyed ogre, who kept roaring like an elephant.

Etto and JoJo lost each other, but their monsters were not so terrible. This kind of monster was created in the subconscious of a brave person who had no monster hidden in their mind. These ogres did not look so evil. This enabled the two friends to beat them without any support, as everybody had to fight alone.

The monster dwelling
in a person's mind
is implanted there from their childhood
and
stays with them until adulthood.

A child who is
brought up properly
and receives plenty of good advice
will become a thoughtful adult.

A child who is
brought up cruelly and always hears rude
and violent words,
Will grow up to be an adult who has evil thoughts.

Imaginary Monster

Imaginary Monster

The screams of fear mixed with the sounds of people running and fighting from many thousands of people could be heard from morning till afternoon. Then, the confusion began to fade away.

The dense fog slowly melted away until everyone could see their fellow travelers. Each person was drenched in sweat from hours of heavy fighting.

After the battle, many of the people had run away. In the beginning, 100,000 people had entered the land of the dreadful ogres, but half had run away. The remaining 50,000 walked into the city of monsters. Finally, after the fog had lifted, only 10,000 people remained.

They aimed to leave the land of monsters before sunset, so that they would be far away from it when nightfall arrived.

The 10,000 people rushed out of the city of the dreadful ogres and everyone had left it before sundown. On their way to the north, they found many stone tablets.

TABLET 4
Five out of ten people quit
their dreams easily.
They think about
their dreams
but never pursue them.
Half of all people quit chasing
their dreams out of fear.
When fear conquers the mind,
people start to imagine things.
They always picture the things
they fear in many forms.
They will think about the danger
before they actually face it.
Finally, there remains
only one person out of ten
who can defeat the obstacles
of their imagination.
The God of Fortune

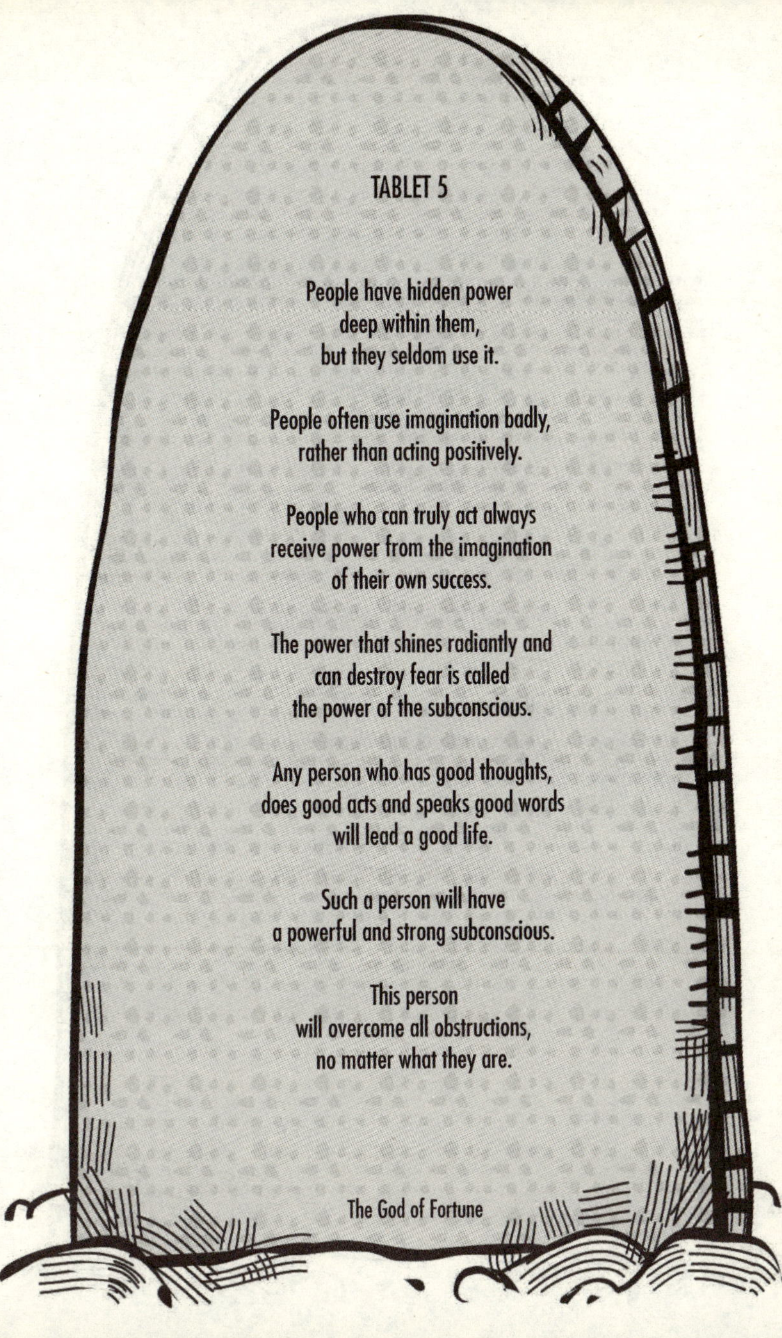

TABLET 5

People have hidden power
deep within them,
but they seldom use it.

People often use imagination badly,
rather than acting positively.

People who can truly act always
receive power from the imagination
of their own success.

The power that shines radiantly and
can destroy fear is called
the power of the subconscious.

Any person who has good thoughts,
does good acts and speaks good words
will lead a good life.

Such a person will have
a powerful and strong subconscious.

This person
will overcome all obstructions,
no matter what they are.

The God of Fortune

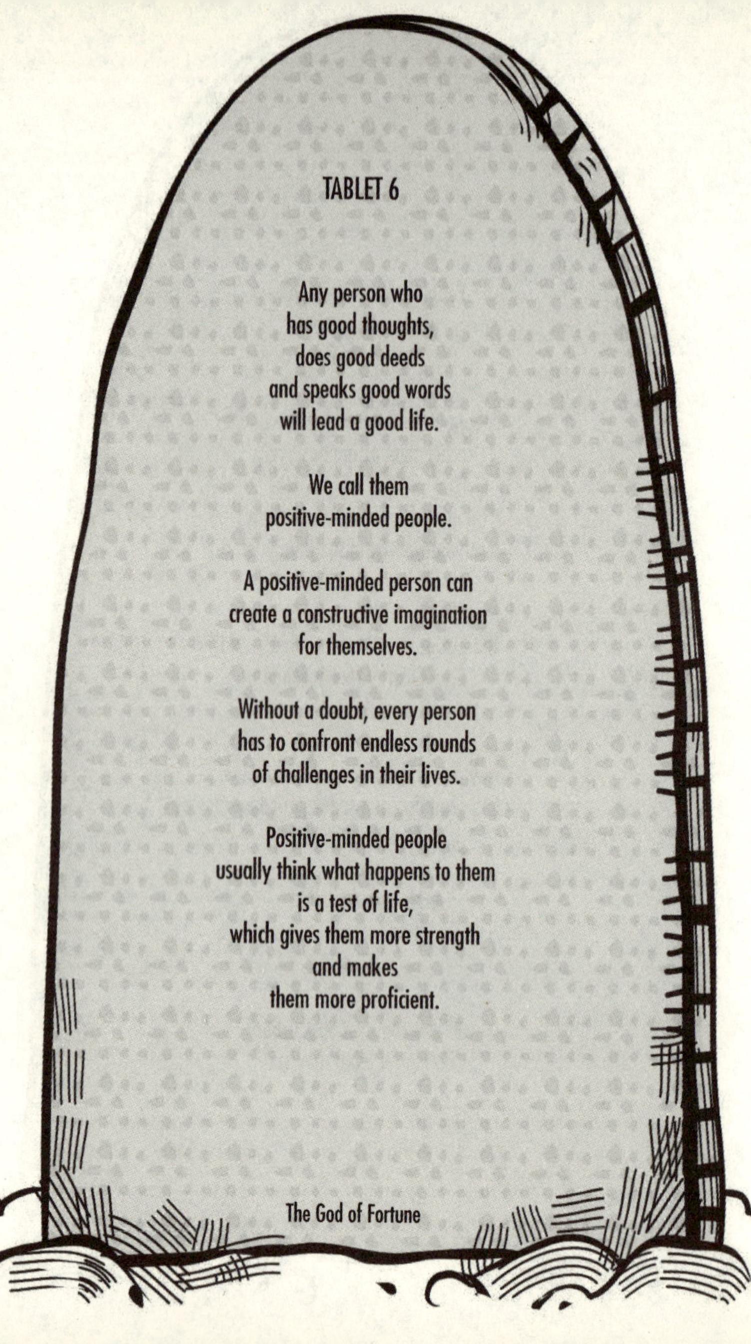

TABLET 6

Any person who
has good thoughts,
does good deeds
and speaks good words
will lead a good life.

We call them
positive-minded people.

A positive-minded person can
create a constructive imagination
for themselves.

Without a doubt, every person
has to confront endless rounds
of challenges in their lives.

Positive-minded people
usually think what happens to them
is a test of life,
which gives them more strength
and makes
them more proficient.

The God of Fortune

Imaginary
Monster

TABLET 7
People always have to
fight their own fears.
Sometimes they win;
sometimes they lose.
People with a strong mind
can always defeat the evil giant
dwelling in their minds.
For people with a weak heart,
the giant will consume
the beauty of their mind,
until none is left within.
Such people will become
a body without a soul,
liveliness or happiness.
What remains in them
is only a wicked mind.
The God of Fortune

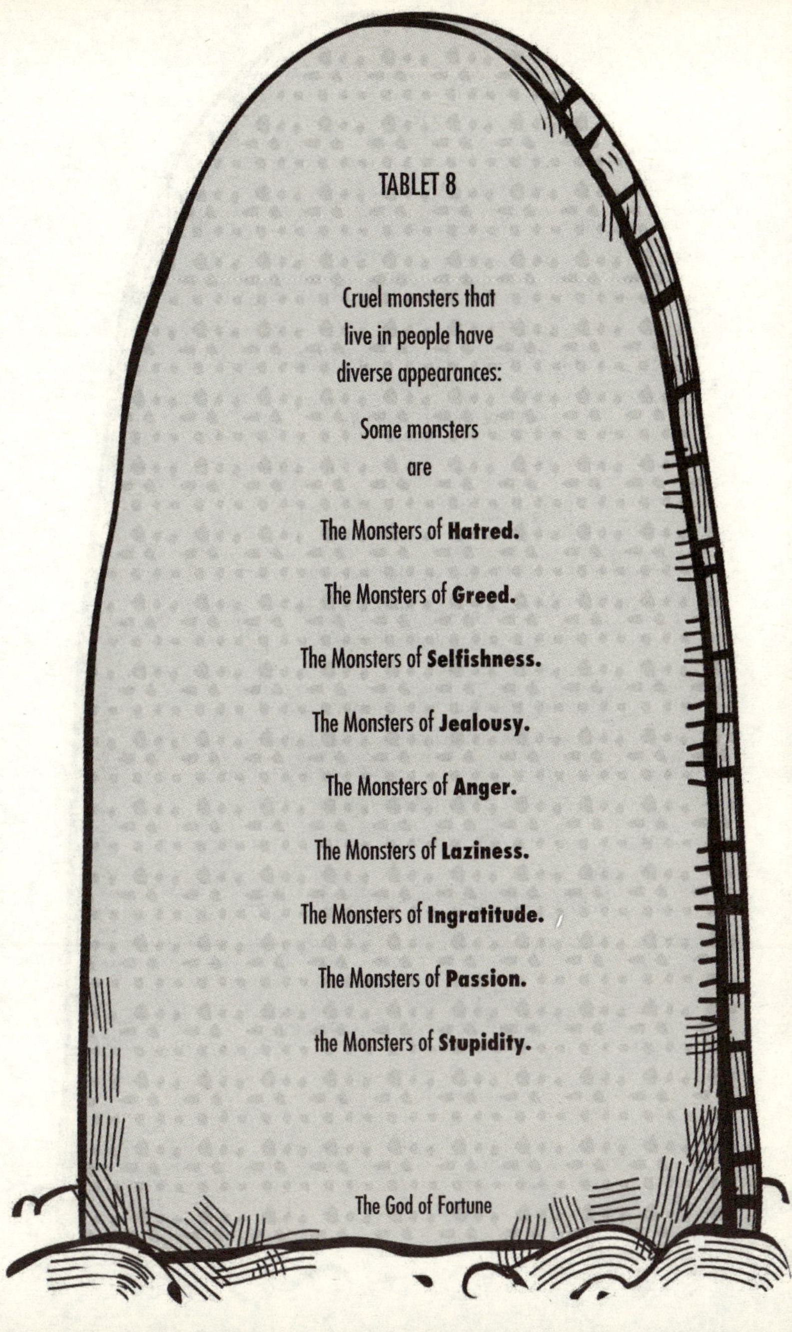
TABLET 8
Cruel monsters that
live in people have
diverse appearances:
Some monsters
are
The Monsters of **Hatred.**
The Monsters of **Greed.**
The Monsters of **Selfishness.**
The Monsters of **Jealousy.**
The Monsters of **Anger.**
The Monsters of **Laziness.**
The Monsters of **Ingratitude.**
The Monsters of **Passion.**
the Monsters of **Stupidity.**
The God of Fortune

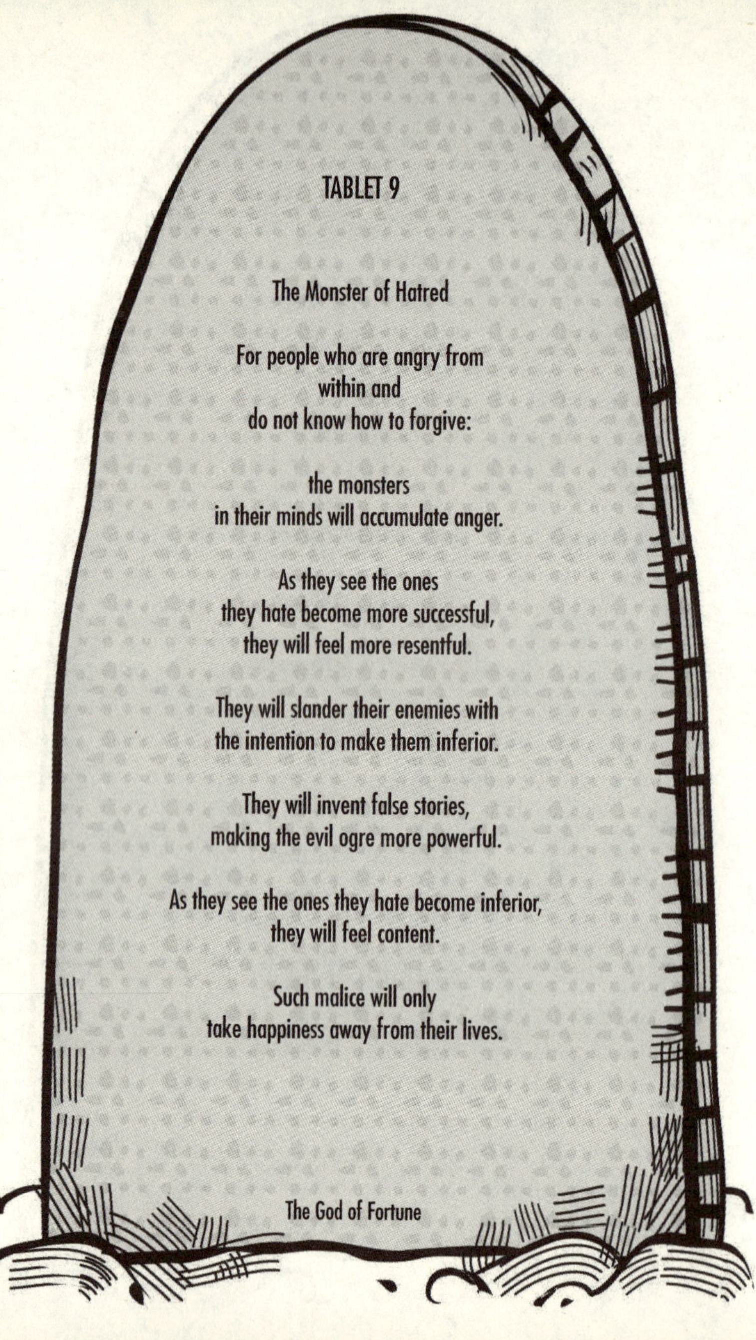
TABLET 9
The Monster of Hatred
For people who are angry from
within and
do not know how to forgive:
the monsters
in their minds will accumulate anger.
As they see the ones
they hate become more successful,
they will feel more resentful.
They will slander their enemies with
the intention to make them inferior.
They will invent false stories,
making the evil ogre more powerful.
As they see the ones they hate become inferior,
they will feel content.
Such malice will only
take happiness away from their lives.
The God of Fortune

Imaginary Monster

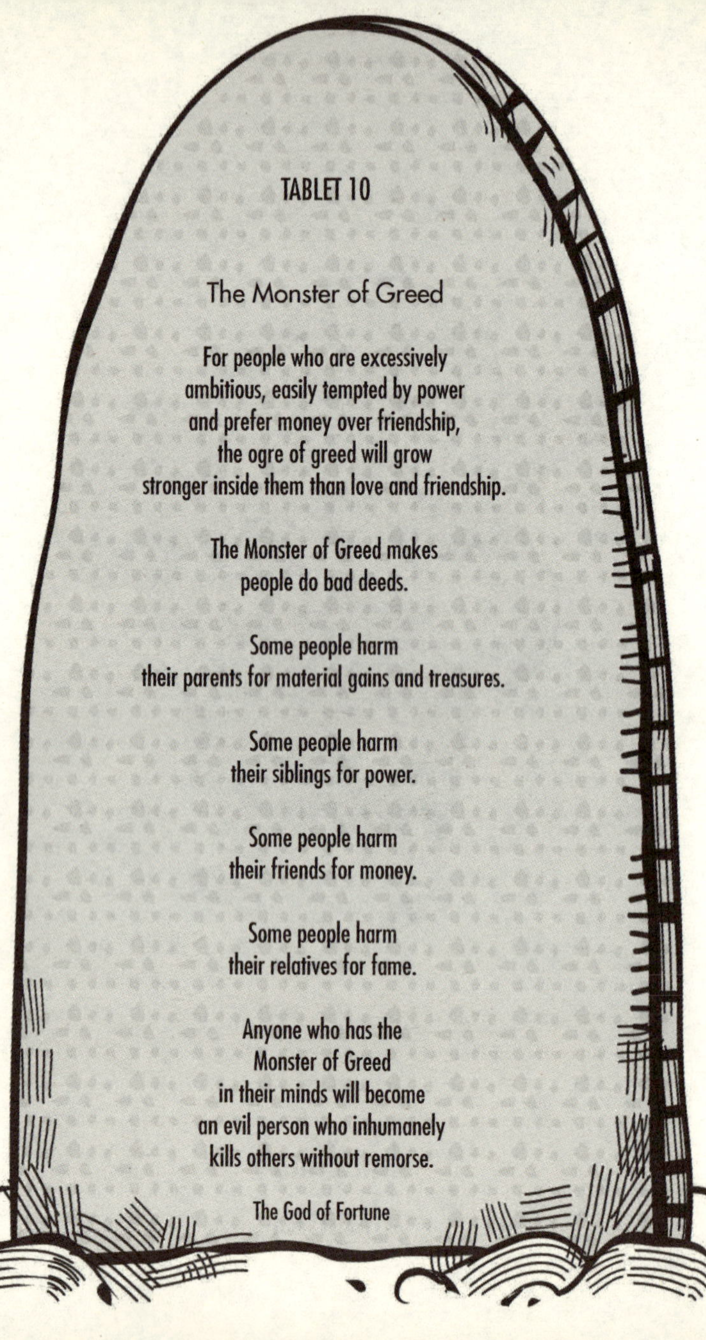

TABLET 10

The Monster of Greed

For people who are excessively
ambitious, easily tempted by power
and prefer money over friendship,
the ogre of greed will grow
stronger inside them than love and friendship.

The Monster of Greed makes
people do bad deeds.

Some people harm
their parents for material gains and treasures.

Some people harm
their siblings for power.

Some people harm
their friends for money.

Some people harm
their relatives for fame.

Anyone who has the
Monster of Greed
in their minds will become
an evil person who inhumanely
kills others without remorse.

The God of Fortune

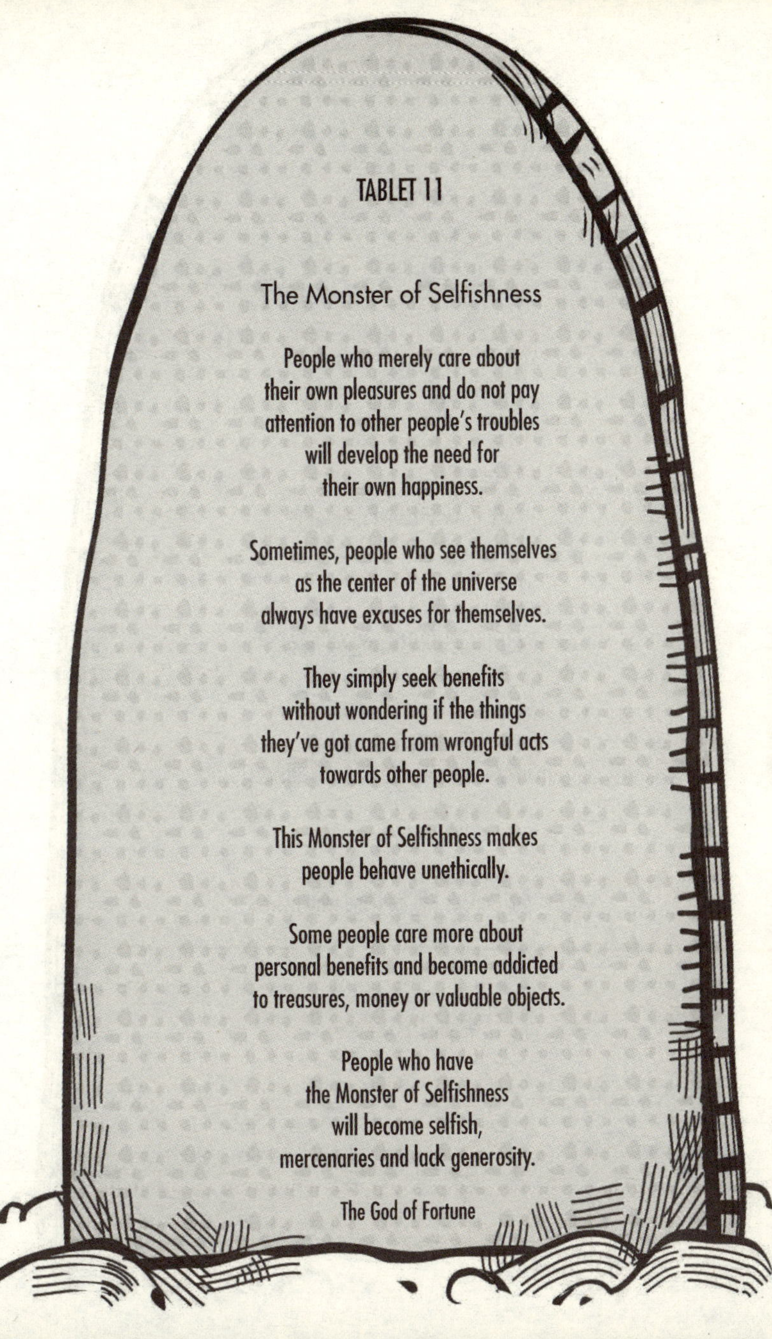

TABLET 11

The Monster of Selfishness

People who merely care about
their own pleasures and do not pay
attention to other people's troubles
will develop the need for
their own happiness.

Sometimes, people who see themselves
as the center of the universe
always have excuses for themselves.

They simply seek benefits
without wondering if the things
they've got came from wrongful acts
towards other people.

This Monster of Selfishness makes
people behave unethically.

Some people care more about
personal benefits and become addicted
to treasures, money or valuable objects.

People who have
the Monster of Selfishness
will become selfish,
mercenaries and lack generosity.

The God of Fortune

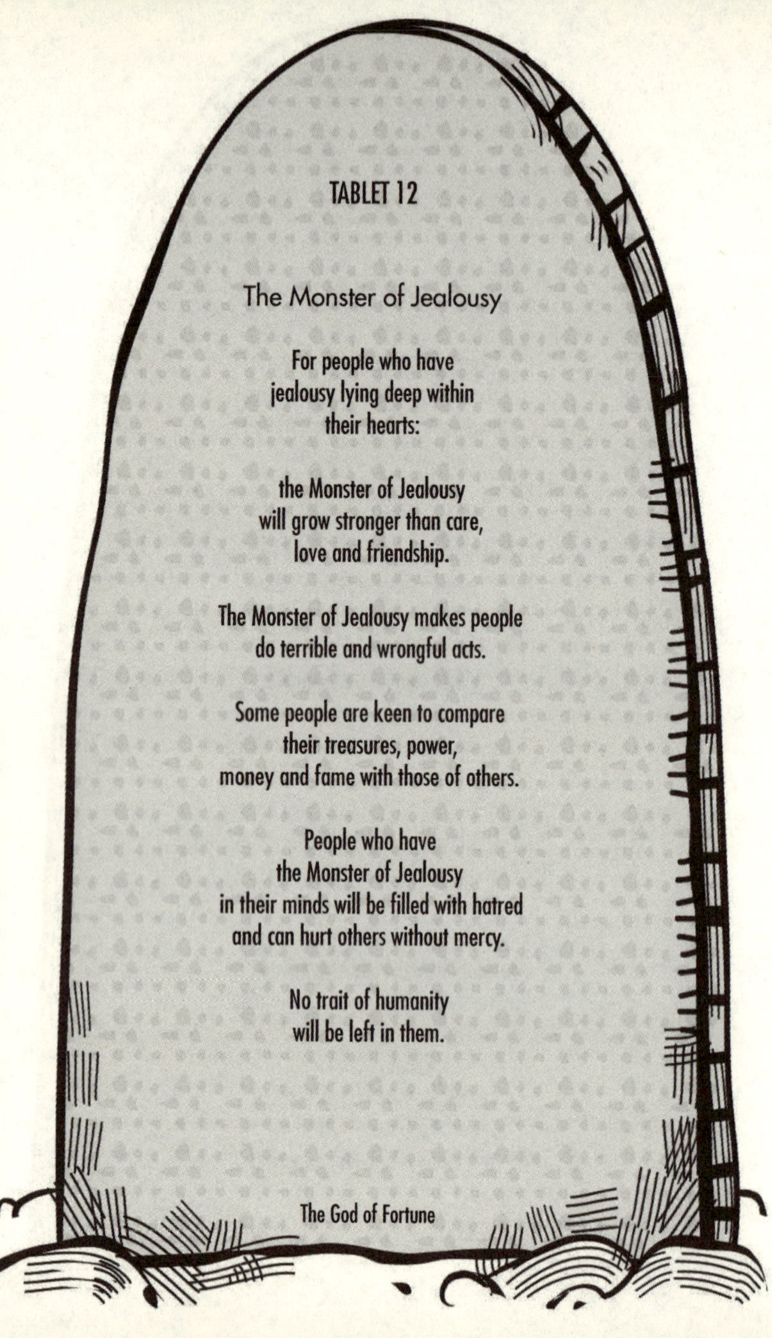

TABLET 12

The Monster of Jealousy

For people who have
jealousy lying deep within
their hearts:

the Monster of Jealousy
will grow stronger than care,
love and friendship.

The Monster of Jealousy makes people
do terrible and wrongful acts.

Some people are keen to compare
their treasures, power,
money and fame with those of others.

People who have
the Monster of Jealousy
in their minds will be filled with hatred
and can hurt others without mercy.

No trait of humanity
will be left in them.

The God of Fortune

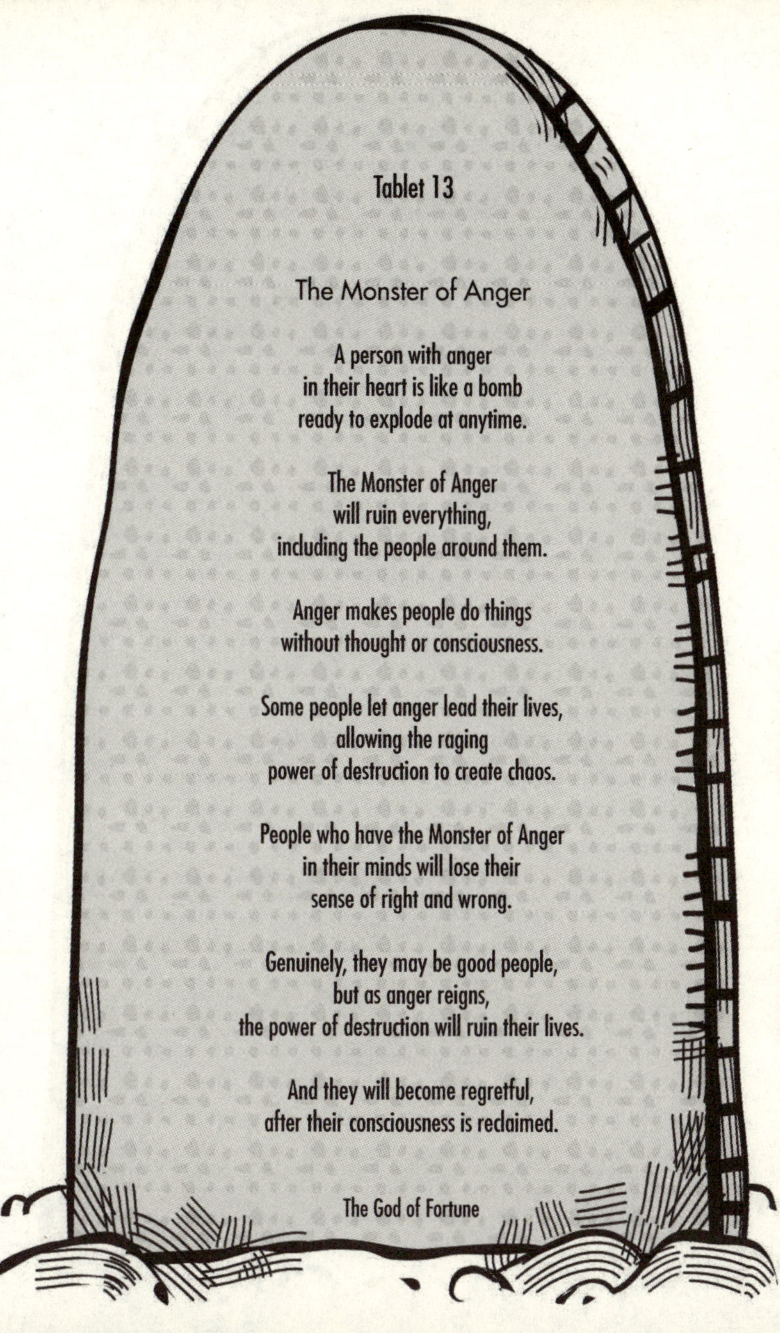

Tablet 13

The Monster of Anger

A person with anger
in their heart is like a bomb
ready to explode at anytime.

The Monster of Anger
will ruin everything,
including the people around them.

Anger makes people do things
without thought or consciousness.

Some people let anger lead their lives,
allowing the raging
power of destruction to create chaos.

People who have the Monster of Anger
in their minds will lose their
sense of right and wrong.

Genuinely, they may be good people,
but as anger reigns,
the power of destruction will ruin their lives.

And they will become regretful,
after their consciousness is reclaimed.

The God of Fortune

TABLET 14

The Monster of Laziness

For people who are lazy
and not interested in work,
the Monster of Laziness
will make their lives fall apart.

The Monster of Laziness
stops people from doing things
they should do,
while encouraging them to do
what they should not.

Some people spend
their lives worthlessly, not knowing
what they want to do.

People who have
the Monster of Laziness
in their minds will become
extremely lazy.

When people ignore work,
learning and education,
they will not realize
the importance
and the value of their lives.

The God of Fortune

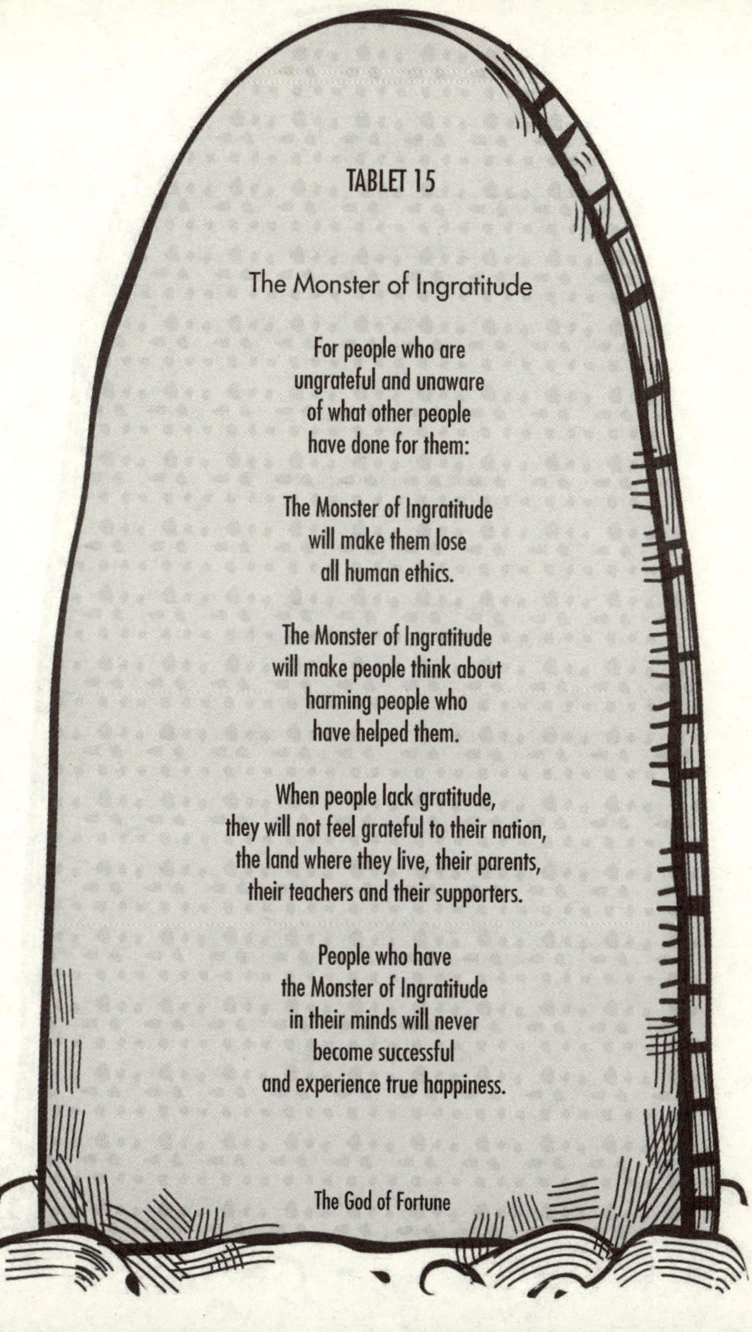

TABLET 15

The Monster of Ingratitude

For people who are
ungrateful and unaware
of what other people
have done for them:

The Monster of Ingratitude
will make them lose
all human ethics.

The Monster of Ingratitude
will make people think about
harming people who
have helped them.

When people lack gratitude,
they will not feel grateful to their nation,
the land where they live, their parents,
their teachers and their supporters.

People who have
the Monster of Ingratitude
in their minds will never
become successful
and experience true happiness.

The God of Fortune

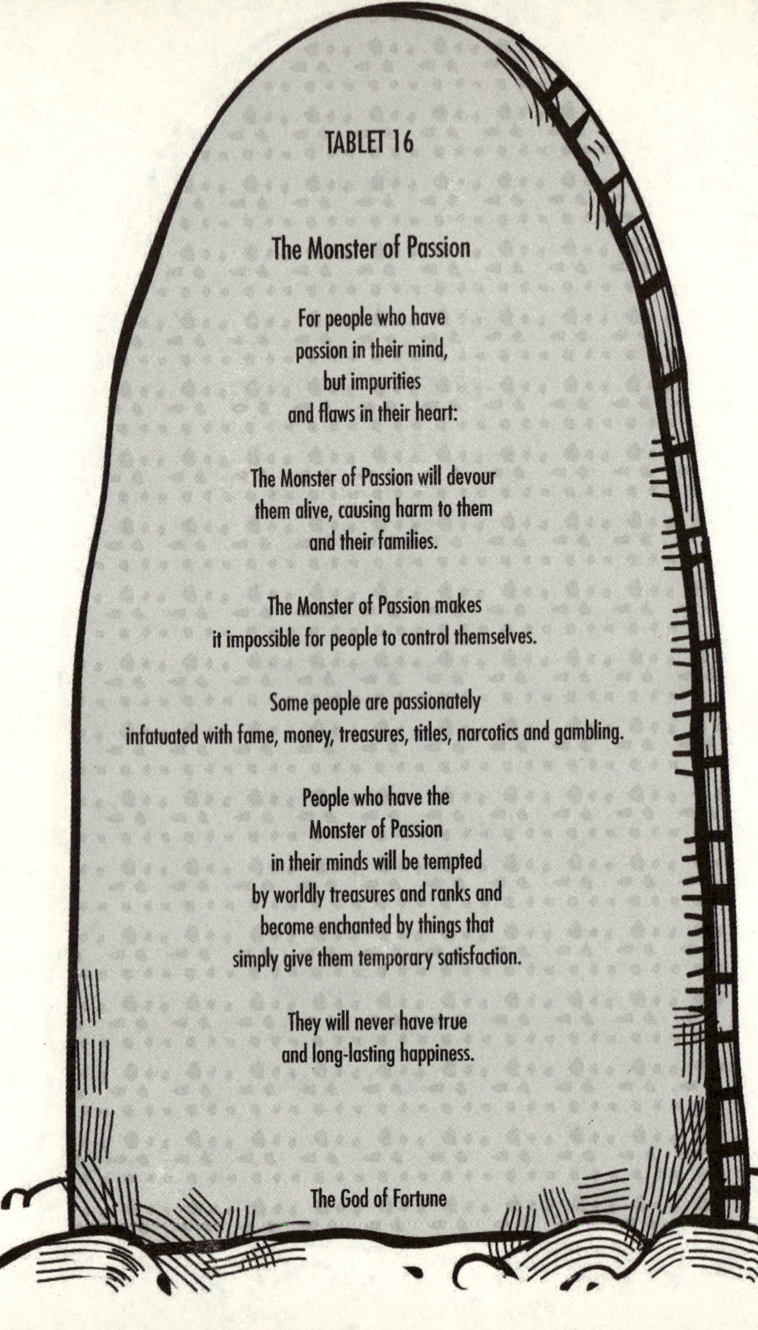

TABLET 16

The Monster of Passion

For people who have
passion in their mind,
but impurities
and flaws in their heart:

The Monster of Passion will devour
them alive, causing harm to them
and their families.

The Monster of Passion makes
it impossible for people to control themselves.

Some people are passionately
infatuated with fame, money, treasures, titles, narcotics and gambling.

People who have the
Monster of Passion
in their minds will be tempted
by worldly treasures and ranks and
become enchanted by things that
simply give them temporary satisfaction.

They will never have true
and long-lasting happiness.

The God of Fortune

TABLET 17

The Monster of Stupidity

People who are
foolish and filled with
imbecilic thoughts,
the Monster of Stupidity
makes them commit mistakes
unknowingly.

The Monster of Stupidity makes
people do things they should not do.

People who do not try to learn
and seek knowledge
will become foolish.

People who have
the Monster of Stupidity in their minds
will behave wrongly while thinking
they are doing right.
Their imbecilic mind causes them
to make mistakes out of ignorance.

Nonetheless, they are not considered
innocent because of their ignorance,
but because of their limited knowledge.

So, they always make mistake and
hype small issues into serious ones.

The God of Fortune

4

Endurance

After they survived the city of monsters, which was all in their minds, JoJo, Etto and 10,000 others walked along the rows of stone tablets and read the inscriptions.

They all learned that the ogres they saw came entirely from their own imagination and subconscious.

People who are actually unkind and pessimistic might appear to be kind-hearted and elegant in appearance. But, in fact, within the mind and the brain of each person was a different experience.

What was hidden in each person's heart was invisible to other people. However, when people experience a period of loneliness, the hidden things in their mind claimed existence without their awareness.

The 10,000 people who survived continued on their journey along their chosen route.They journeyed on and on until they reached a desert. Here, the heat became more fierce and each of them began to feel thirsty.

Still, they marched on. Even though many drank a lot of water during the journey, their thirst doubled under the heat. They were extremely thirsty, but they had exhausted their last reserves of water three days ago.

Lack of food and water while being in the hot desert made many of them weak. Many of them had prepared food in advance, but did not have enough resources when they needed them the most.

Many people do not
think and plan in advance.

They simply like to
fix problems at hand.

To simply fix problems at hand
means not
having a plan for their lives.

Many people are doomed
to fail because
they do not have a plan.

A large number of people began to succumb to the harshness of walking through the desert without enough food and water. They fell to the ground under the scorching sun.

These young people had survived many dangers, but they could not withstand a body that was unhealthy and lacking in energy.

Some saved energy by drinking and eating less, as they did not know when they would be able to refill on food and water. So, they consumed their supplies economically. Those who fell to the ground did so because of lack of food and water.

A lot of people dropped away from the group, but the rest continued despite the reduced speed. However, they kept walking one step after another.

People who plan
their lives in advance
always seek to
prevent a problem
before it happens.

Planning is like
foreseeing situations.

A good leader always
makes careful
plans in advance,
both for his work
and personal life.

We must move forward.

No matter what happens,
we have to let our lives go on.

Some of the people began
to see mirages in the desert.

These mirages occurred
as the sunlight reflected off the sand
at a distance and was reflected into
their eyes as an image.

Some saw a water resource,
like an oasis or a lake,
while others saw food.

But as they walked
closer and closer,
nothing they had seen could be found.

All they saw was emptiness.

When people need
something badly,
they see things
differently from the truth.

Most people consider
the things they want
as good things and
what other people want
as nonsense.

Therefore, many people
are keen to look down on
other people's thoughts,
needs and dreams.

But those who look down on others
do not realize that the things
they want are merely illusions.

The number of people
who fell to the sand increased
from one to ten, then a 100,
a 1,000 and finally, many thousands.

This made the group
thin out in numbers and become separated.

Less and less people
survived their time in the sun-scorched desert.

Finally, there were only
a 1,000 people left out of
the original 10,000
who had entered this land.

People who use their
resources economically
will have resources left
for the future.

Some people use
resources wastefully
without preparing
supplies for the future.

These people will not
have what they need
when it is absolutely necessary.

On the night of the seventh day, only a 1,000 people had survived their time in the desert.

As they reached the edge of the desert, a strange phenomenon occurred. They saw the adjacent land was a dense forest.

Suddenly, it began raining heavily. The group of people shouted in delight, as they had not come across any water for quite a long time.

Some people shed tears of extreme joy. Their endurance had enabled them to overcome a number of obstacles. People began hugging one another while thinking about the hardships they had suffered and the struggles they had overcome together.

The world does not
change at all.

It is human endurance
that becomes less.

Human endurance varies.

Some people are strong
and
have a large body,
but cannot withstand difficulties.

Some people are thin
and fragile,
but can withstand
a lot of hardship.

Human endurance
can be divided in two parts:

physical endurance
and
mental endurance.

Some people
seem to have remarkable
physical endurance,
but they have less mental endurance.

Some people
seem to have remarkable mental endurance,
but as they face testing situations,
they might not be able to
control their minds
and they let the pressure get to them.

The more facilities
we invent for
our comfort,
the less endurance we have.

People may not be
aware that their
endurance lessens,
until they face
serious situations.

We then realize that
our endurance has receded.

After they reached the end of the land that connected the desert and the thick forest, someone yelled that he had seen another stone tablet.

He asked his fellow travelers to come forward and read the stone tablet. JoJo and Etto, the two loving friends, who had journeyed through the desert together, ran through the rain to read the tablet together with the other 1,000 people.

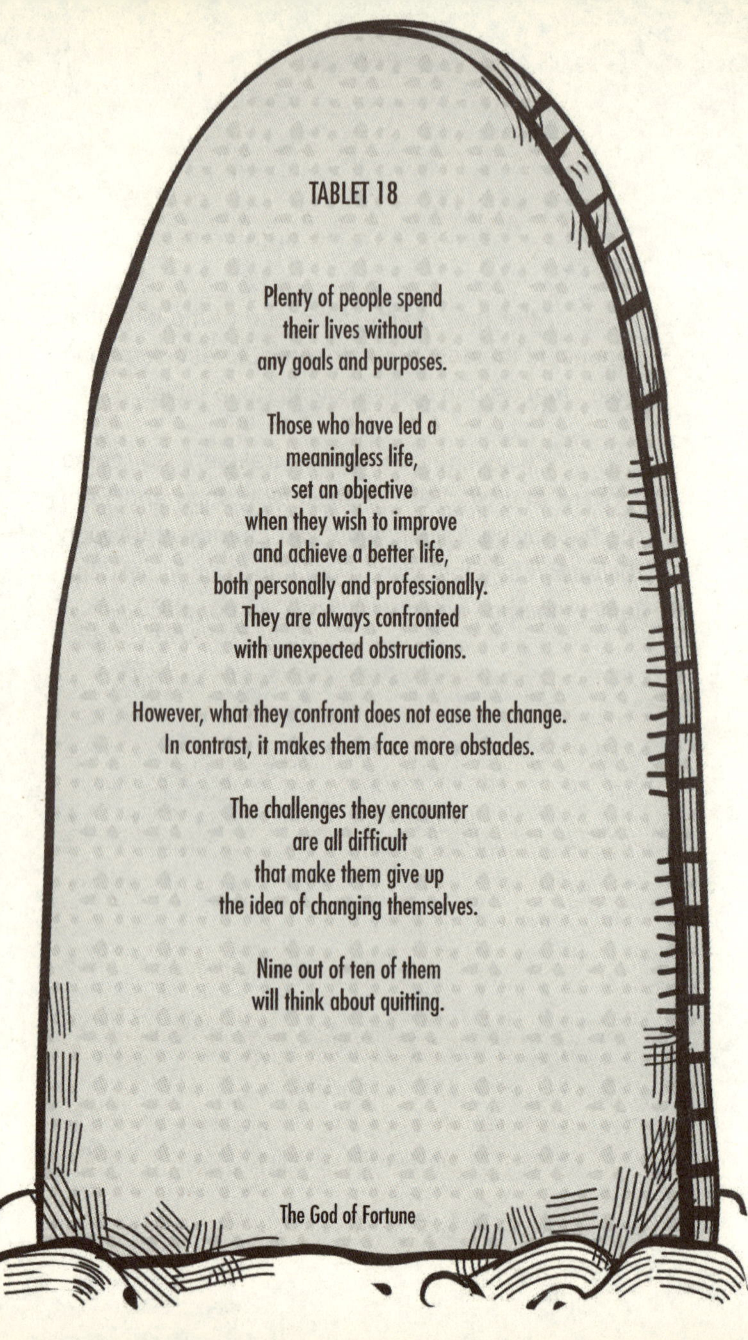

TABLET 18

Plenty of people spend
their lives without
any goals and purposes.

Those who have led a
meaningless life,
set an objective
when they wish to improve
and achieve a better life,
both personally and professionally.
They are always confronted
with unexpected obstructions.

However, what they confront does not ease the change.
In contrast, it makes them face more obstacles.

The challenges they encounter
are all difficult
that make them give up
the idea of changing themselves.

Nine out of ten of them
will think about quitting.

The God of Fortune

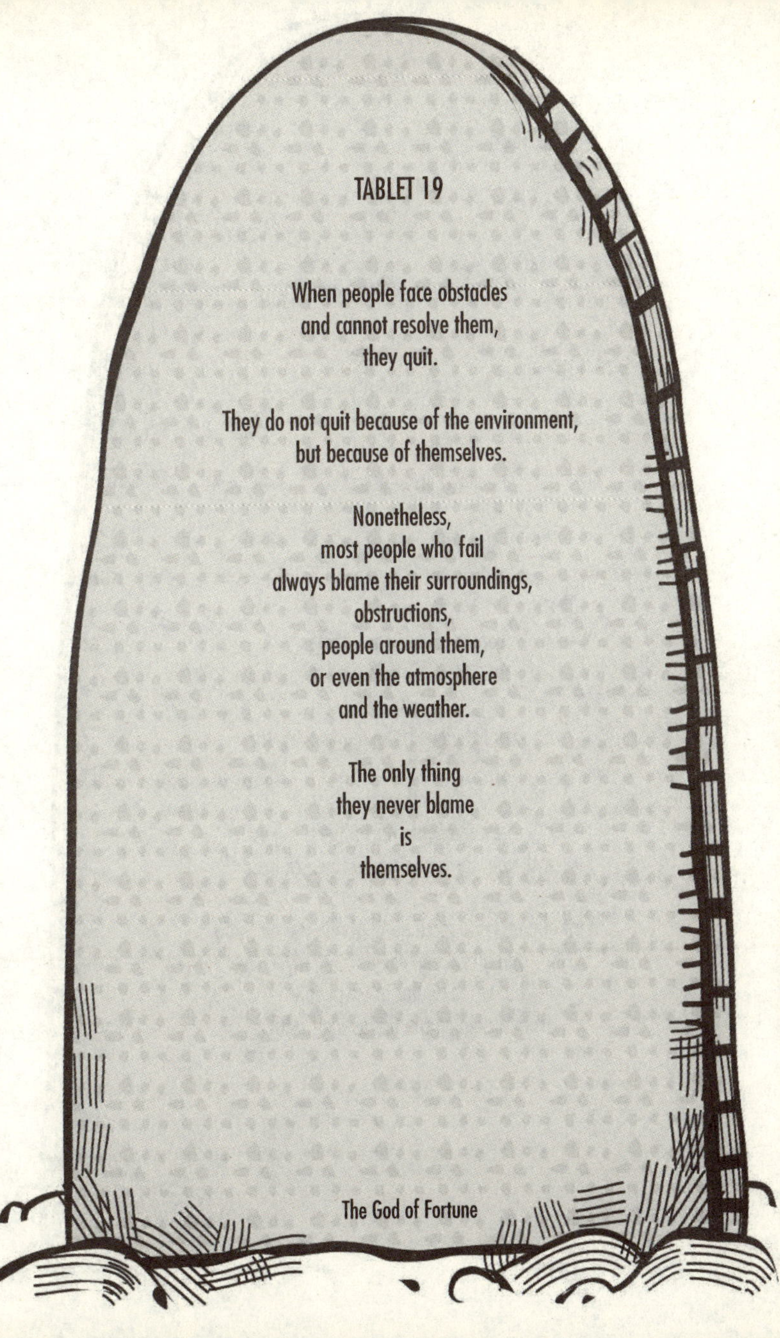

TABLET 19

When people face obstacles
and cannot resolve them,
they quit.

They do not quit because of the environment,
but because of themselves.

Nonetheless,
most people who fail
always blame their surroundings,
obstructions,
people around them,
or even the atmosphere
and the weather.

The only thing
they never blame
is
themselves.

The God of Fortune

Tablet 20
People learn to have needs.
Some people
have beautiful dreams.
Some people
have great dreams.
But everything a person
wants does not always come easily.
People always want things
they do not have
and
are dissatisfied with the things they do.
Worse than that,
some people hurt others
with vile words and despicable actions.
A lot of people do manage to obtain the pleasant
and nice things they dream of,
but try to hinder other people
from obtaining the things they want.
The God of Fortune

5

Alternatives

The remaining 1,000 people walked into the dense forest. They had all passed the tests by the God of Fortune, but only one among them would defeat all the obstacles. The God of Fortune would decide to stay with that one all through his life.

Many people had died along the journey and others had dropped out. This had filled fear in the hearts of so many. Many people confronted obstacles and were eager to face more of them as they realized there was no way to escape. These obstructions were no coincidences; they were a part of life. If we avoid them today, we will have to face them another day in the future.

Most people run away
and
do not dare face
the obstacles in their lives.

No matter whether
such obstacles
are severe or not,
people find ways
to escape and stay away
from them.

But people don't understand
that the obstacles
don't disappear.
They can only flee
from them for a while.

Sooner or later,
they come back.

Only the brave
who dare confront troubles,
will survive.

The ones who accept
that they have limited capabilities
and
are not born with talents,
realize that
they have no special abilities,
so try to practice, fight, confront,
as well as accept the truth.
These people will then possess a stronger mind
and will be able to better face their challenges.

A person who thinks,
speaks and does well
will have a strong mind,
since goodwill prevents
evil from overwhelming this Earth.

The 1,000 people entered the forest full of bindweed one after another. They could not see very far because the bindweed was too dense.

Those who walked in front had to chop down giant leaves, climbers and other plants that obstructed the path of the group.

They soon reached a foothill where the earth was divided into around ten openings that looked like small caves. These were only wide enough for one person to enter.

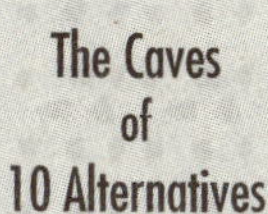

The Caves of 10 Alternatives

There are many ways for people to choose.
Divide into groups of even quantity.

Then, choose one from
the ten paths to journey on
to find what you long for.

Alternative 1	Money
Alternative 2	Gold
Alternative 3	Power
Alternative 4	Treasures
Alternative 5	Blessedness
Alternative 6	Family
Alternative 7	Health
Alternative 8	Wealth
Alternative 9	Work
Alternative 10	Happiness

Whichever path you choose to walk,
always head towards the end.

Only then will you find what you desire.

The God of Fortune

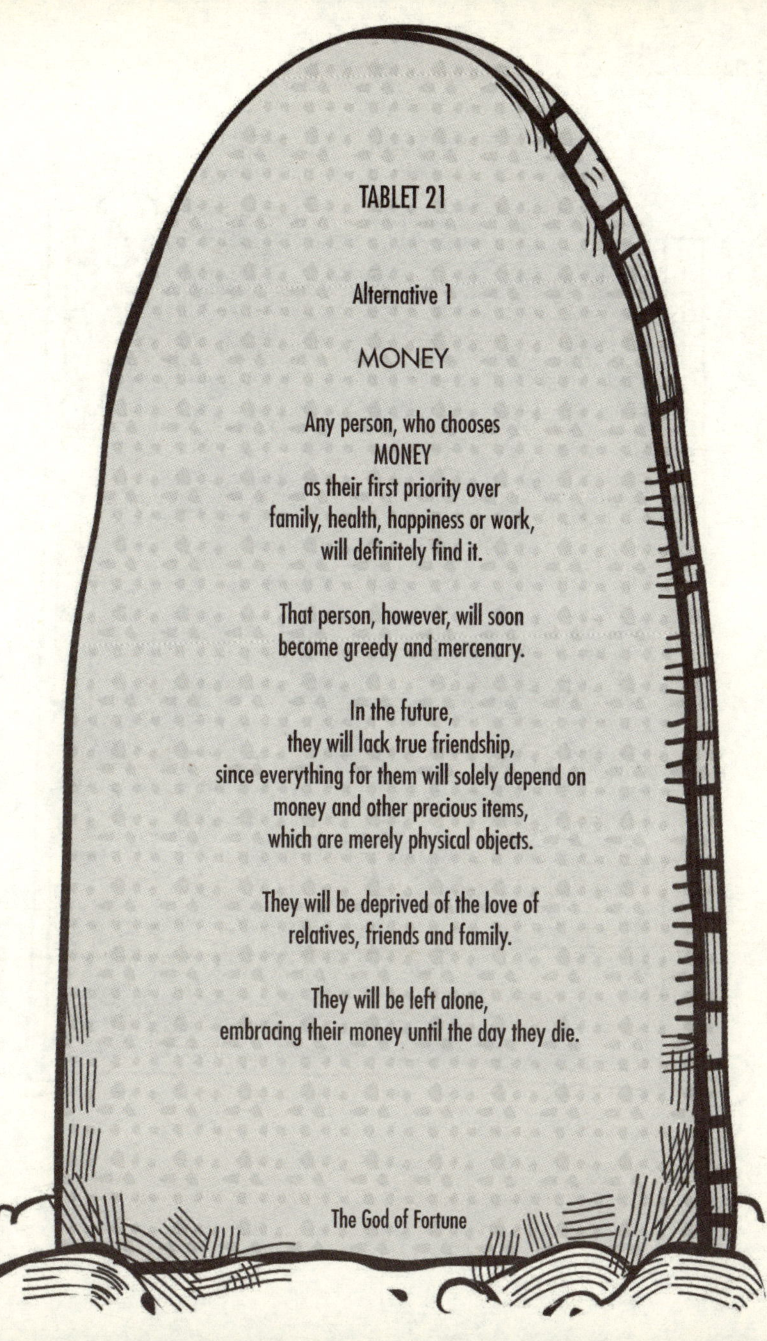

TABLET 21

Alternative 1

MONEY

Any person, who chooses
MONEY
as their first priority over
family, health, happiness or work,
will definitely find it.

That person, however, will soon
become greedy and mercenary.

In the future,
they will lack true friendship,
since everything for them will solely depend on
money and other precious items,
which are merely physical objects.

They will be deprived of the love of
relatives, friends and family.

They will be left alone,
embracing their money until the day they die.

The God of Fortune

Gold

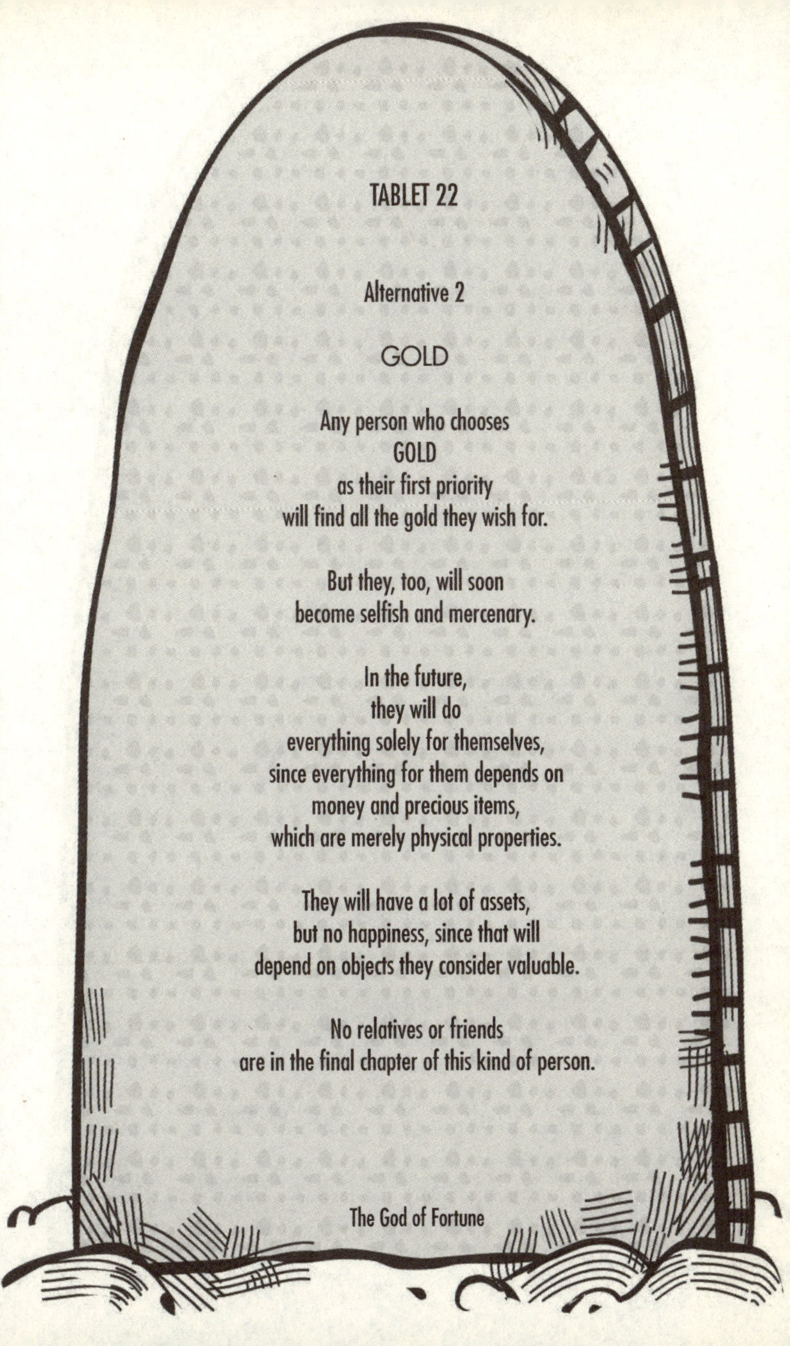

TABLET 22

Alternative 2

GOLD

Any person who chooses
GOLD
as their first priority
will find all the gold they wish for.

But they, too, will soon
become selfish and mercenary.

In the future,
they will do
everything solely for themselves,
since everything for them depends on
money and precious items,
which are merely physical properties.

They will have a lot of assets,
but no happiness, since that will
depend on objects they consider valuable.

No relatives or friends
are in the final chapter of this kind of person.

The God of Fortune

TABLET 23

Alternative 3

POWER

Any person who chooses
POWER
as their first priority
will find all the power they wish for.

But they will become
addicted to power and abuse it.

Most people who choose power are
always tempted by it
to such an extent that they forget that
goodness used to be a great ideal.

Use of power to kill fellow humans.

Use of power to suppress those
who disagree.

Finally, people will curse, object and oppose.
There will be nothing left
in the final phase of their lives.

The God of Fortune

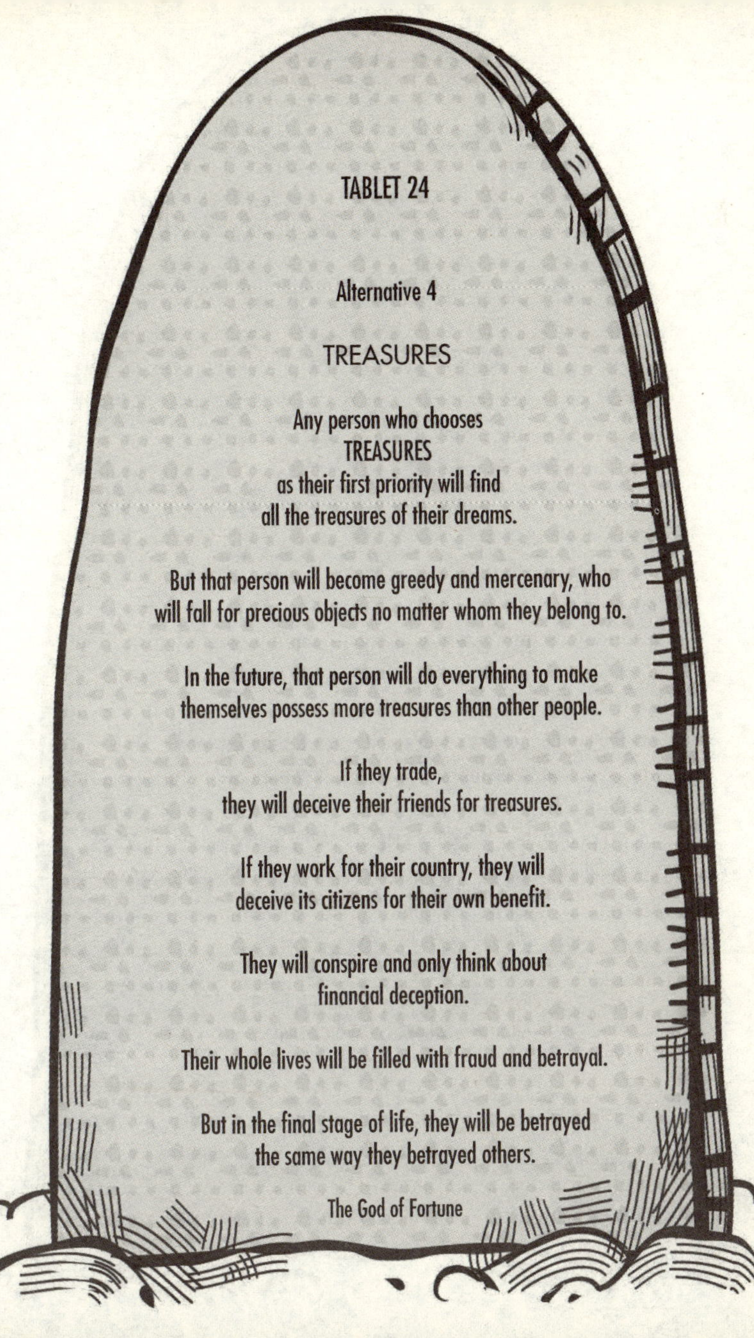

TABLET 24

Alternative 4

TREASURES

Any person who chooses
TREASURES
as their first priority will find
all the treasures of their dreams.

But that person will become greedy and mercenary, who will fall for precious objects no matter whom they belong to.

In the future, that person will do everything to make themselves possess more treasures than other people.

If they trade,
they will deceive their friends for treasures.

If they work for their country, they will deceive its citizens for their own benefit.

They will conspire and only think about financial deception.

Their whole lives will be filled with fraud and betrayal.

But in the final stage of life, they will be betrayed the same way they betrayed others.

The God of Fortune

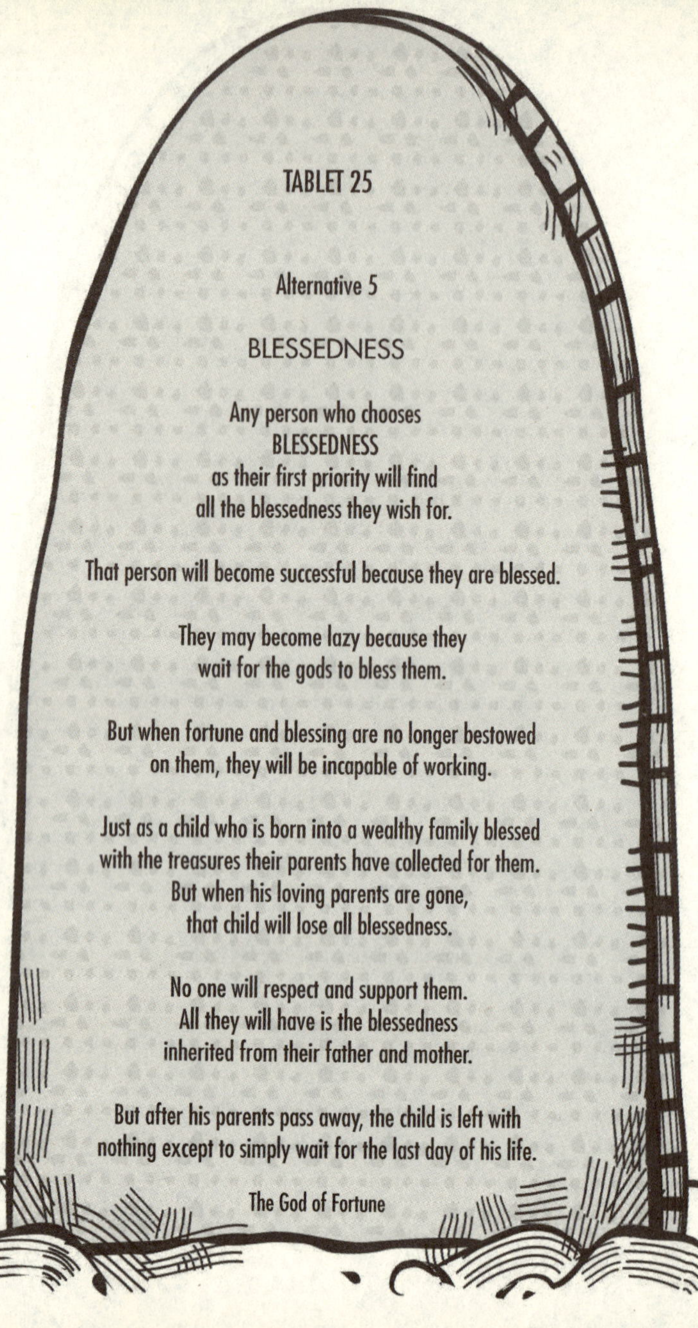

TABLET 25

Alternative 5

BLESSEDNESS

Any person who chooses
BLESSEDNESS
as their first priority will find
all the blessedness they wish for.

That person will become successful because they are blessed.

They may become lazy because they
wait for the gods to bless them.

But when fortune and blessing are no longer bestowed
on them, they will be incapable of working.

Just as a child who is born into a wealthy family blessed
with the treasures their parents have collected for them.
But when his loving parents are gone,
that child will lose all blessedness.

No one will respect and support them.
All they will have is the blessedness
inherited from their father and mother.

But after his parents pass away, the child is left with
nothing except to simply wait for the last day of his life.

The God of Fortune

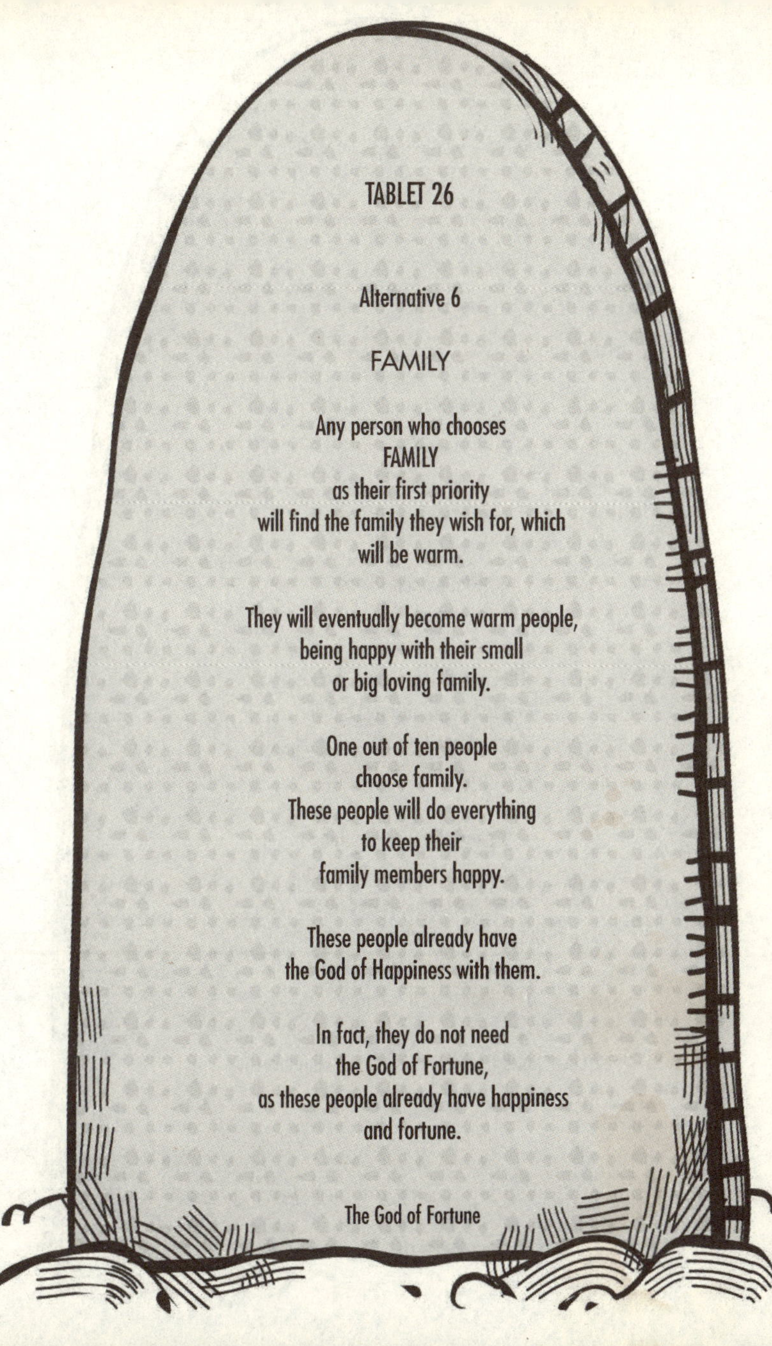

TABLET 26

Alternative 6

FAMILY

Any person who chooses
FAMILY
as their first priority
will find the family they wish for, which
will be warm.

They will eventually become warm people,
being happy with their small
or big loving family.

One out of ten people
choose family.
These people will do everything
to keep their
family members happy.

These people already have
the God of Happiness with them.

In fact, they do not need
the God of Fortune,
as these people already have happiness
and fortune.

The God of Fortune

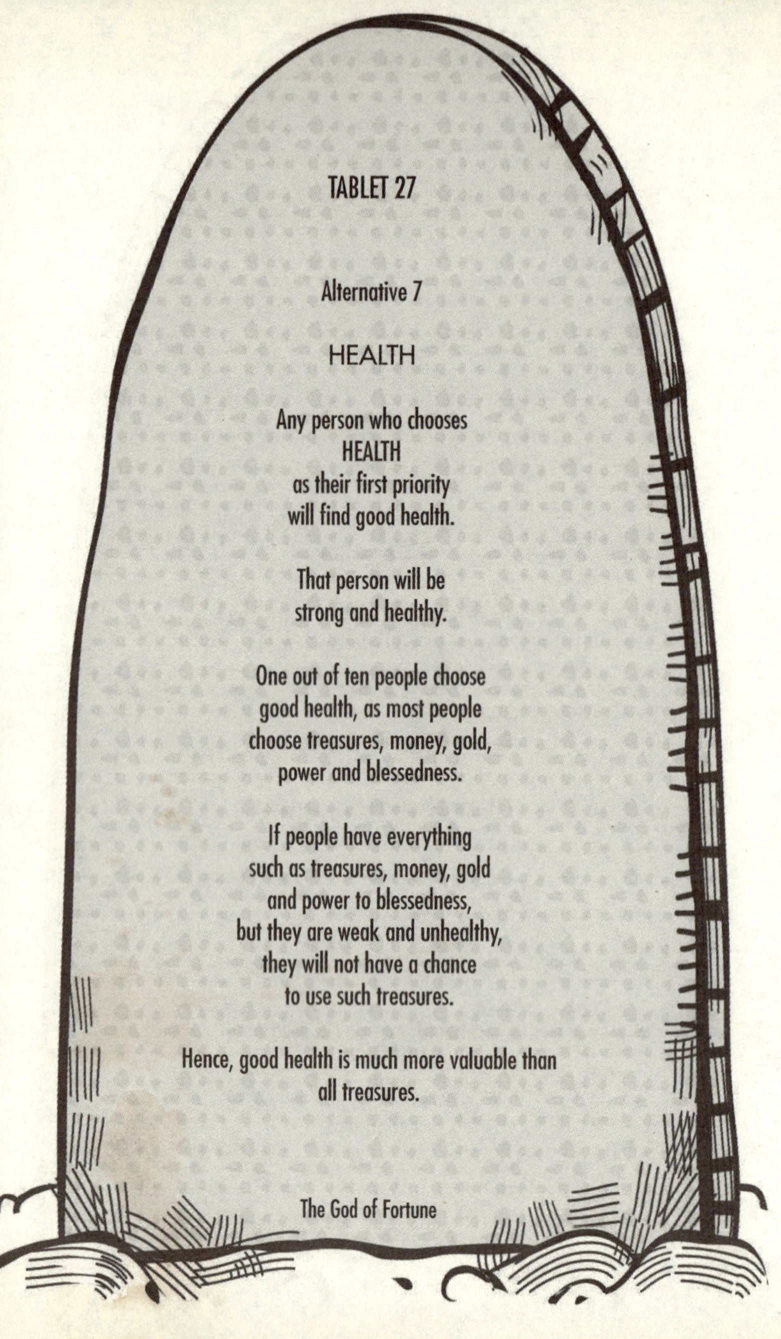

TABLET 27

Alternative 7

HEALTH

Any person who chooses
HEALTH
as their first priority
will find good health.

That person will be
strong and healthy.

One out of ten people choose
good health, as most people
choose treasures, money, gold,
power and blessedness.

If people have everything
such as treasures, money, gold
and power to blessedness,
but they are weak and unhealthy,
they will not have a chance
to use such treasures.

Hence, good health is much more valuable than
all treasures.

The God of Fortune

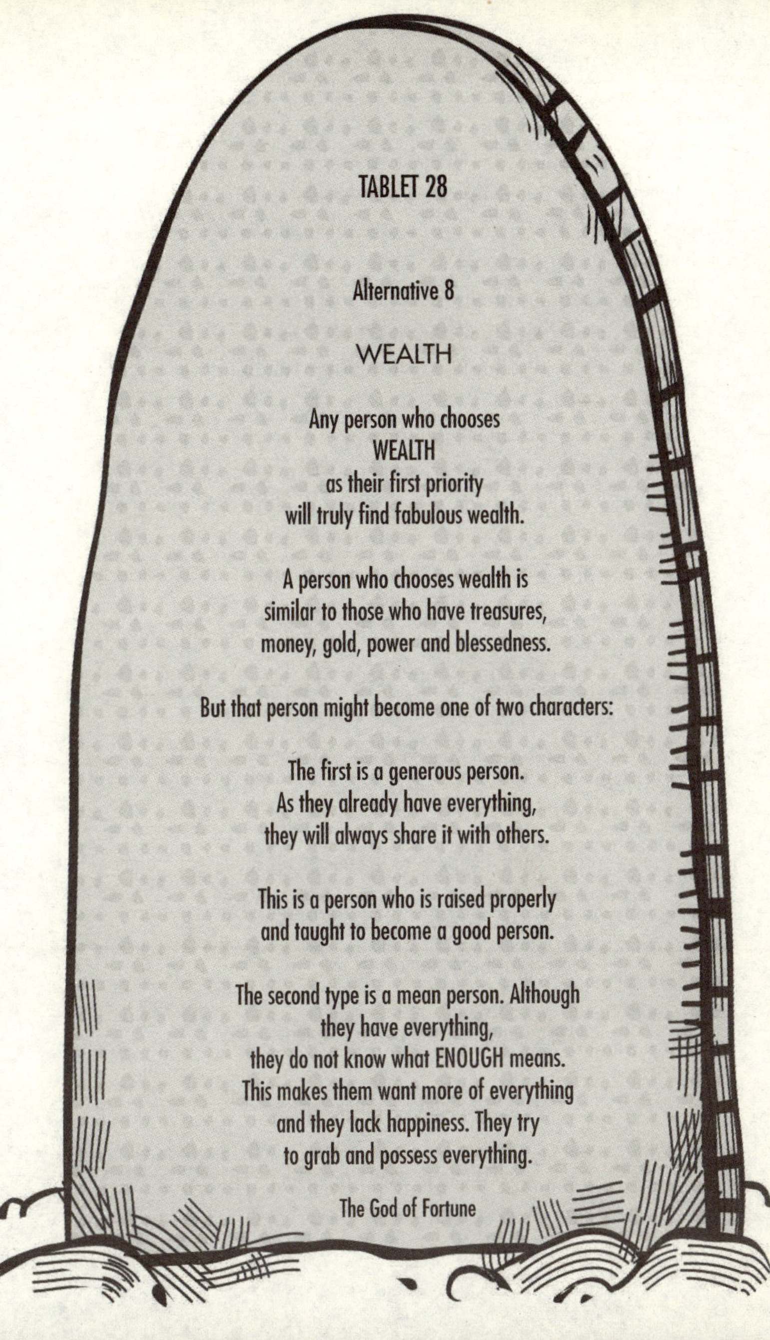

TABLET 28

Alternative 8

WEALTH

Any person who chooses
WEALTH
as their first priority
will truly find fabulous wealth.

A person who chooses wealth is
similar to those who have treasures,
money, gold, power and blessedness.

But that person might become one of two characters:

The first is a generous person.
As they already have everything,
they will always share it with others.

This is a person who is raised properly
and taught to become a good person.

The second type is a mean person. Although
they have everything,
they do not know what ENOUGH means.
This makes them want more of everything
and they lack happiness. They try
to grab and possess everything.

The God of Fortune

Not many people
take care of their health.
They will realize the downside after it is too late.

They will become aware,
as they are pained to death that
they just want to recover from illness.

But there is no way out.
There is no way to cure them
but to go to the doctors.

The money they have been collecting
will be spent for medical treatment.

Take care of yourself more.
Eat vegetables, fruits and fish.
Be happy with good food
at reasonable prices.

Stop seeking expensive but poisonous food.

Raw meat with red flesh
always makes us sick.

It will become poisonous and dangerous.

It is harmful and will make us sad.

It will make us suffer to death.

If you love your life and your health,
take care of it.

Whether you are a child
or an adolescent,
always examine yourself.
And your health will be fine.

A strong body will bring happiness.

There will be no suffering,
illness or problem.

Happiness will come every day
and all the time.

Be aware of the value of life and destiny.

Gods or holy spirits
should not be blamed for making us sick.

That is not destiny.

Heaven does not make us ill.

But not taking care of our health does.

Exercising and eating good food
will make us happy and give us good health.

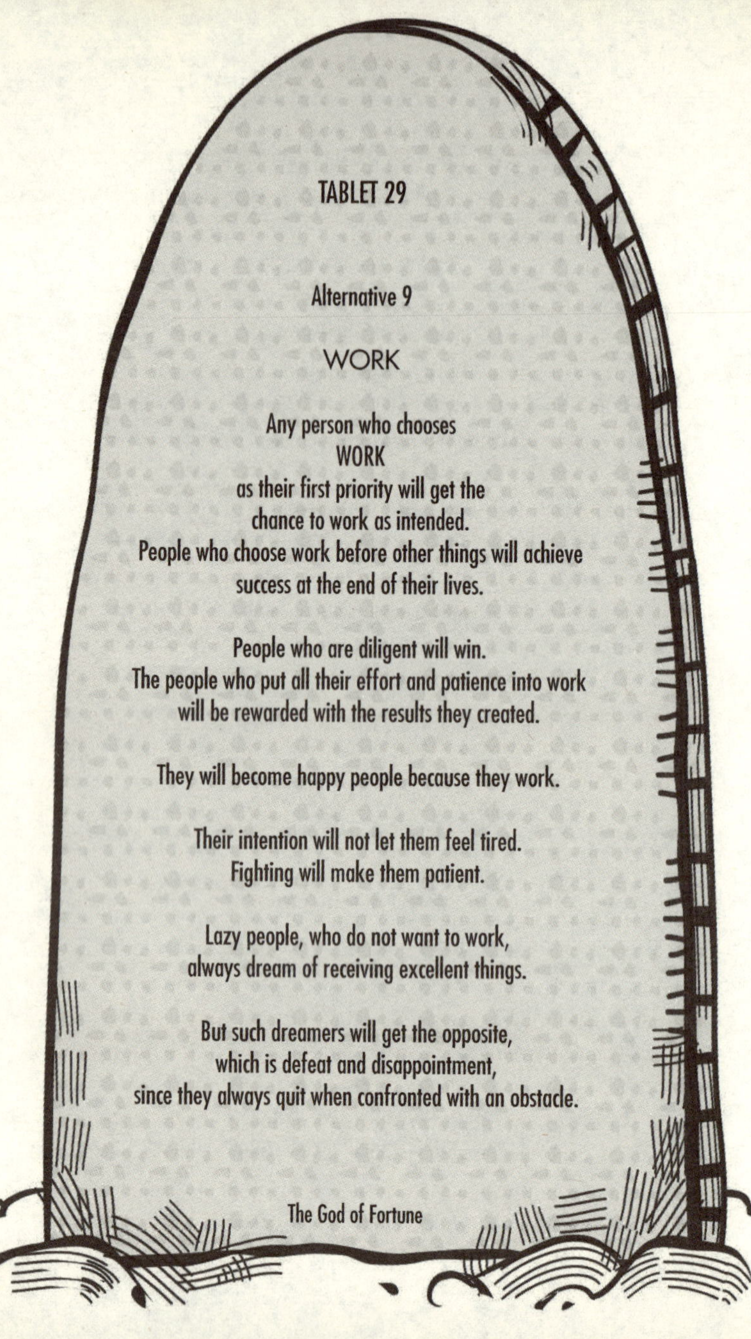

TABLET 29

Alternative 9

WORK

Any person who chooses
WORK
as their first priority will get the
chance to work as intended.
People who choose work before other things will achieve
success at the end of their lives.

People who are diligent will win.
The people who put all their effort and patience into work
will be rewarded with the results they created.

They will become happy people because they work.

Their intention will not let them feel tired.
Fighting will make them patient.

Lazy people, who do not want to work,
always dream of receiving excellent things.

But such dreamers will get the opposite,
which is defeat and disappointment,
since they always quit when confronted with an obstacle.

The God of Fortune

TABLET 30

Alternative 10

HAPPINESS

Any person who chooses
HAPPINESS
as their first priority
will absolutely find true happiness.

That person will remain happy all the time.

Whether they are poor or rich,
they will always be happy
if they simply find happiness
in their own minds.

Only one out of ten choose happiness.

Most people always choose treasures,
money, gold, power and blessedness.

But they do not know that physical objects,
no matter how abundant,
cannot buy happiness.

Fortunate people, who do not need to
depend on the God of Fortune, are
the ones who choose the path of happiness.

The God of Fortune

Happiness

Money

Many people
search for
the things they want.

Some fail
and
others succeed.

People have different needs.

People who achieve
what they want have to
experience plenty of
issues in life.

There are both
good and bad stories,
together with happiness,
sadness, satisfaction
and separation.

Each holds true in life.

A true life is not a perfect life
filled with everything.

A true life is one that
throws in many obstacles for us to face.

If we compare life with food,
someone who confronts nothing
and leads a simple life
until they die is like insipid food,
which is unappetizing.

Someone who has to overcome
obstacles and experience
happiness, satisfaction,
disappointment, discouragement
and sadness is like colorful
and appetizing food which
contains a burst of flavors.

Its various colors and appetizing tastes always make
us feel excited and stimulated.

6

Swords

The 1,000 people divided themselves into ten groups of a 100 people each and entered the ten caves.

Each group was blessed by the God of Fortune to find the things they wanted and were all satisfied. They found an exit soon after they had located the things they desired hidden in the caves.

As each of them reached the exit, a white beam flashed brightly and they had to shut their eyes. When they opened their eyes, the friends they had entered the caves with were gone.

They were all returned to their villages by the magical power of the God of Fortune.

Apart from the others, many people were sent home along with their treasures, money and power. However, there was one group of people that was not sent home.

All the groups of people who had chosen money, gold, power, treasures, blessedness, family, health, wealth and happiness were transported to their villages, except the group that chose the Cave of Work.

It seemed that every person who chose the **Cave of Work** would have to face more hardships. While most people already had everything they wanted, these 100 people would now have to carry on their journey because they were willing to work.

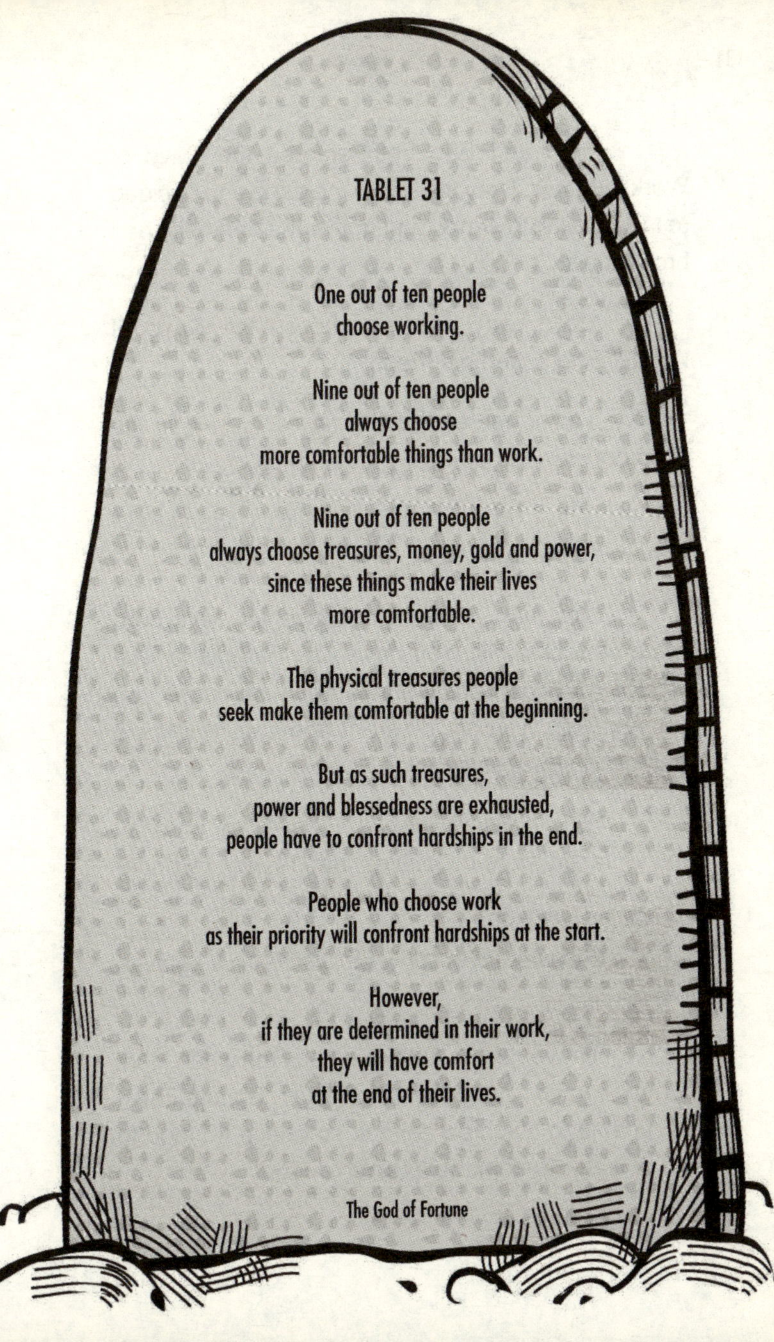

TABLET 31

One out of ten people
choose working.

Nine out of ten people
always choose
more comfortable things than work.

Nine out of ten people
always choose treasures, money, gold and power,
since these things make their lives
more comfortable.

The physical treasures people
seek make them comfortable at the beginning.

But as such treasures,
power and blessedness are exhausted,
people have to confront hardships in the end.

People who choose work
as their priority will confront hardships at the start.

However,
if they are determined in their work,
they will have comfort
at the end of their lives.

The God of Fortune

JoJo and Etto both entered the Cave of Work together. They walked in the dark, and decided to talk to kill the silence and horror the darkness had brought with it.

"JoJo, why did you choose the Cave of Work?" Etto asked his friend.

"I'm not sure. I think that everything in life does not come to us easily," replied JoJo.

"What do you mean? I don't understand." Etto was curious.

"You may not know because you were born into a perfect family. You have your parents to take care of you. Your family status does not cause you any hardship. You are different from me. You know that, don't you?" said JoJo.

"Yes, I know that you have no parents. You've faced more difficulties than I have. I wonder how you survived."

Etto wanted to know more about his beloved friend.

"I have no one to take care of me when I feel hungry. I have to find food for myself. Sometimes, I am unable to catch an animal, so I have no food to eat or water to drink," explained JoJo.

"Sometimes, when the weather becomes cooler, I have no place to sleep. I have to lay on pile of straw in the barn to survive the night," said JoJo

He continued, When I feel lonely, I want somebody to hug me. But I have no one who can give me love and warmth.

The hardships I have faced in my life have made me realize that if we want anything, we have to *work for it*.

What about you? Why did you choose this path?" JoJo asked Etto.

"I came here because I wanted my family to see that I have capabilities. At home, we have a lot of treasures and money, even more than necessary. My father and mother obtained everything I ever needed since I was a child. I have plenty of things. But all my friends said I was a dependent child who would not be able to survive after my parents die. So, I traveled along with you to prove my bravery," Etto explained.

"I've seen you pass many obstructions already. It is enough to prove your bravery," JoJo said.

"Thank you for the encouragement. I know people who come from a limited status like yours. During the journey, I talked to many people. But a lot of them chose to walk into the Caves of Money, Gold, Power, Treasures, Blessedness and Wealth. Their choices were different. So, I wondered why you chose the Cave of Work," said Etto.

"I don't know. I think every person can choose their own path, because it is their life," replied JoJo.

"But what if the path we've chosen is wrong? What then?" Etto questioned.

"What we can do is understand that our mistakes are important life lessons. We cannot go back to the past and correct things. But we can remember them as lessons throughout our lives," JoJo answered.

"Your answer is very good. I wish to apply it too," Etto complimented his friend.

"Of course, if you see a good thing, then you can adopt it," said JoJo.

Then, they continued on their journey together.

Every person
chooses their own path.

No one forces us
to choose the path we walk.

But when people face failure,
they always blame others
and
everything around them.

Only a few people
own up to their failures.

Only a few people
accept they've made
wrong decisions.

People who are keen
to blame others
do not learn to improve themselves.

They do not know that
those mistakes
will create a lot of benefits
and
become good lessons
to prevent such things
from being repeated in the future.

Therefore,
blaming someone else
does not lead to an advantage,
but
learning from
our mistakes creates
immensely precious lessons.

900 were transported back to their homes by the bright white beam of the God of Fortune.

The people who chose the **Cave of Work** still had to march on. They found a stone tablet with the words **Swords of Survival** written on it.

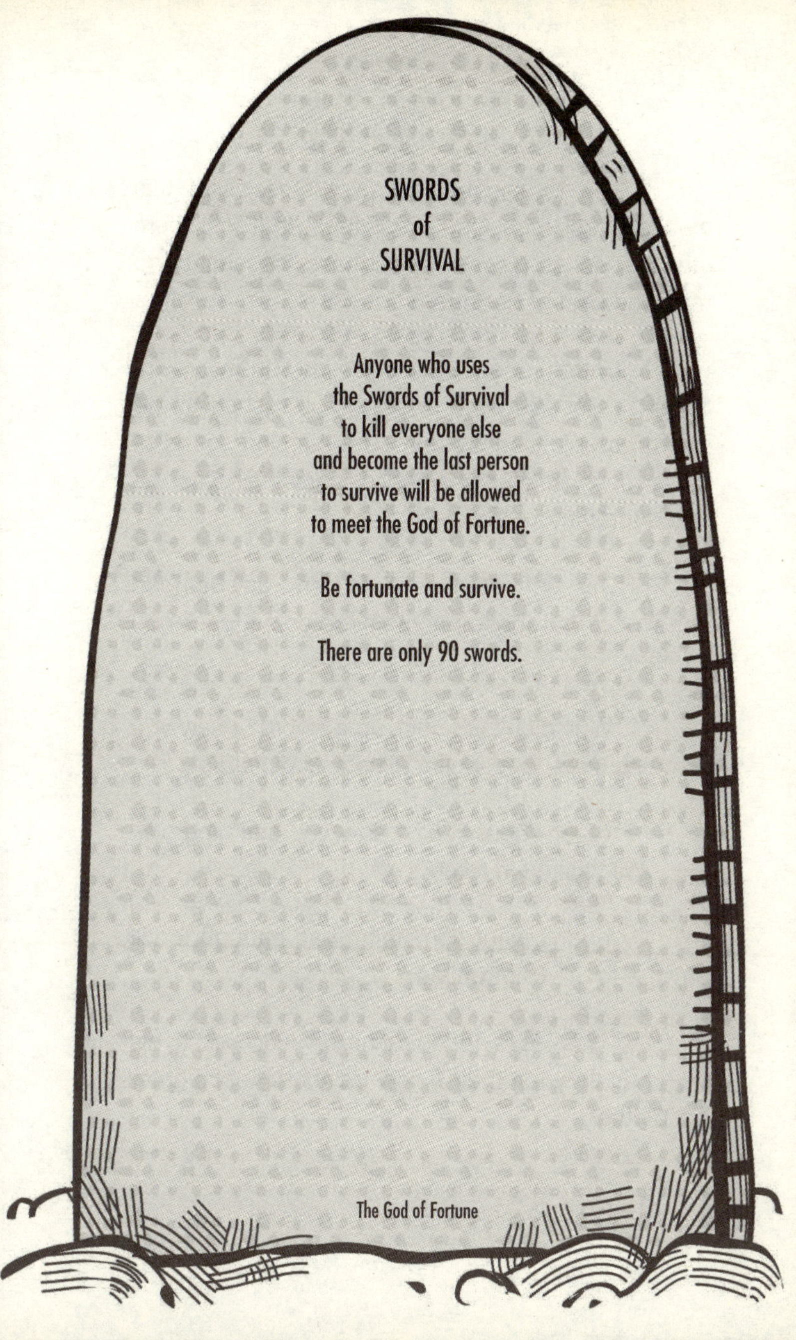
SWORDS
of
SURVIVAL
Anyone who uses
the Swords of Survival
to kill everyone else
and become the last person
to survive will be allowed
to meet the God of Fortune.
Be fortunate and survive.
There are only 90 swords.
The God of Fortune

The remaining 100 people received this message from the God of Fortune, that told them that the last to survive would have the chance to meet the God of Fortune.

Unfortunately, there were only 90 Swords of Survival. So, everyone in the group rushed to the swords and jostled for one. The piercing sound of the swords striking against one another could be heard throughout the cave.

This sight stunned JoJo and Etto. Both did not expect that these people were going to kill one another.

“Why didn’t you pick up a sword? I saw you standing there for a while,” Etto asked JoJo.

“What about you? I saw you standing still, too,” JoJo asked in return.

“I don’t want something bad enough to kill anyone for it,” Etto replied.

“Then, let’s get out of here,” JoJo said to his friend as they left their fellow travelers to slaughter each other.

"Etto persuaded some other friends to come along, too. There were ten of them who did not want to fight with the others.

The ten people out of a 100 walked out of the battlefield where their friends were killing each other in order to meet the God of Fortune.

They decided to give up their right to participate in this competition, because they did not wish to kill or harm anyone.

They did not want to cause anyone undue suffering. They did not want anyone to be injured or to die without having the chance to go home to meet their families.

7

Spoon

The ten who abandoned the **Swords of Survival** intended to begin their journey home. They talked and decided to be friends. They walked away happy, because they thought that all throughout their lives they would never harm anyone, no matter what happened.

The group of ten people did not feel any regret. They all simply walked. Many of them came from different cities. They told the stories of their lives. Each of them was glad and proud of themselves as they were among the last 100 people who might have had the chance to meet the God of Fortune.

The 90 people who were swinging swords to kill one another were in a different state of mind from the ten who were conversing with joy. The 90 men seemed intent in killing their rivals no matter who they were: good or bad people, rich or poor men, noblemen or citizens.

They each thought themselves worthy of becoming the winner and being accepted by the God of Fortune. There would only be one who could kill all his fellow travelers in order to achieve the highest benefit.

The feelings of the two groups were extremely contrasting. One group talked, smiled and laughed while walking.

The other group wanted to kill one another for their own survival. The sound of the swords striking against one another continued unceasingly.

The ten people who were heading home wanted to find something to eat in order to celebrate before they went their separate ways. They helped one another find food.

They walked so far they could no longer hear the fighting. Instead, they heard the sound of a waterfall. So, they decided to go to the waterfall to catch some fish for dinner, which would be the last meal before each began his journey home.

While wading around the waterfall, JoJo saw two huge stone tablets. He called out to Etto and their other friends to come and see.

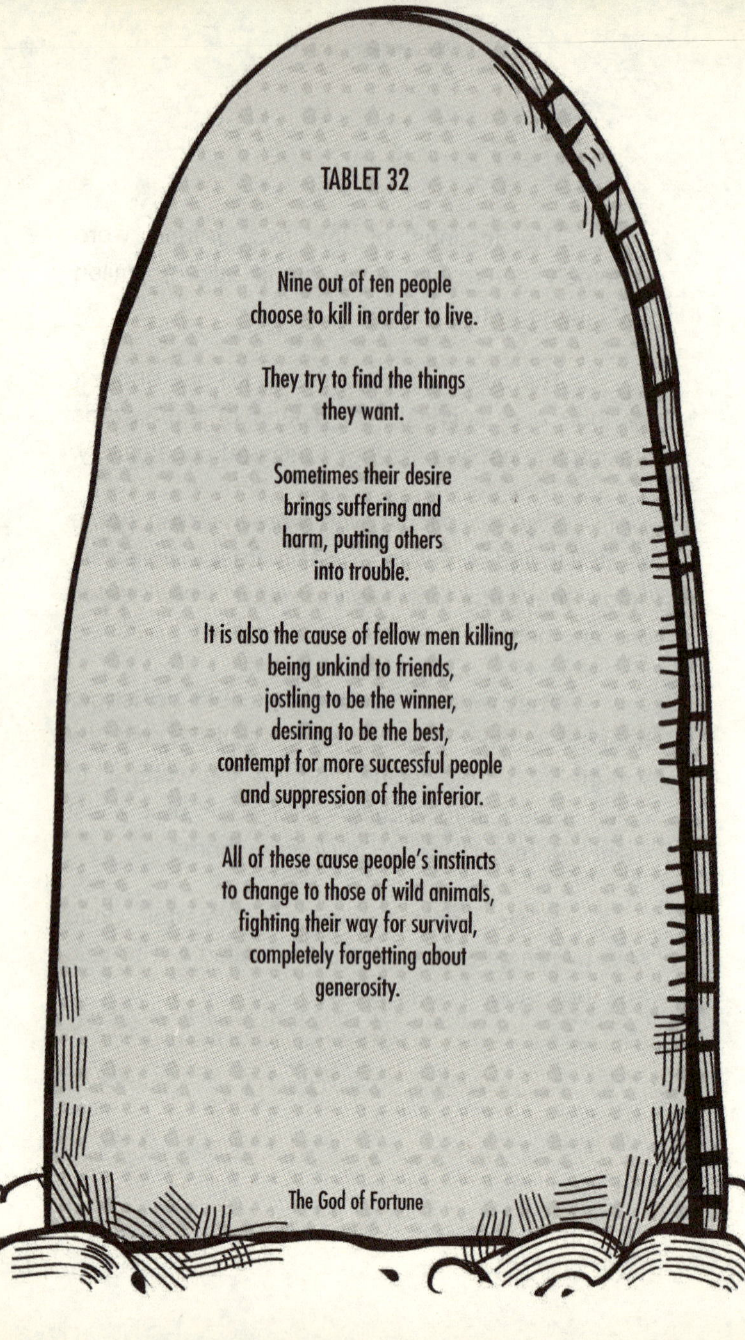

TABLET 32

Nine out of ten people
choose to kill in order to live.

They try to find the things
they want.

Sometimes their desire
brings suffering and
harm, putting others
into trouble.

It is also the cause of fellow men killing,
being unkind to friends,
jostling to be the winner,
desiring to be the best,
contempt for more successful people
and suppression of the inferior.

All of these cause people's instincts
to change to those of wild animals,
fighting their way for survival,
completely forgetting about
generosity.

The God of Fortune

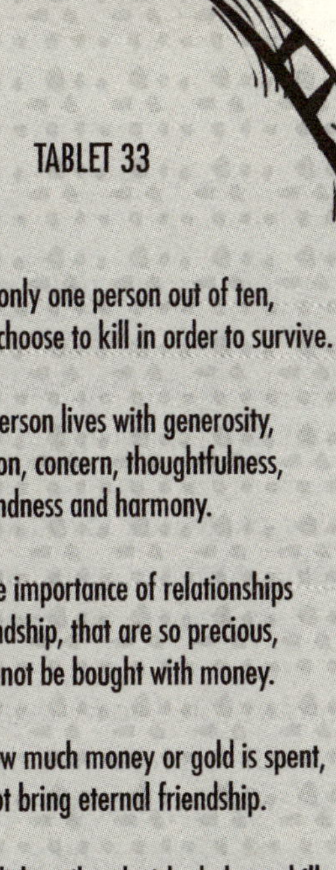

TABLET 33

There is only one person out of ten,
who does not choose to kill in order to survive.

Such a person lives with generosity,
compassion, concern, thoughtfulness,
kindness and harmony.

We see the importance of relationships
and friendship, that are so precious,
they cannot be bought with money.

No matter how much money or gold is spent,
it cannot bring eternal friendship.

The bad, foolish, evil and wicked always kill
their friends and harm their followers.

They curse the bosses who support them.
They do not respect their parents.

They betray friends and are concerned about
their own comfort.
These people have an evil mind.

They will become slaves to their own sins.

The sins they committed against others
will come back to harm them some day.

The God of Fortune

The ten people read through the tablets. However, they did not understand why there were more tablets, because they had already decided not to pick up the swords, giving up their right to fight.

They continued to walk along their chosen route, hoping to find more stone tablets. They completely forgot about their hunger.

They traveled so far away from the waterfall that they could no longer hear its sound. Suddenly, they saw a large cave. At the entrance of the cave, they saw another stone tablet.

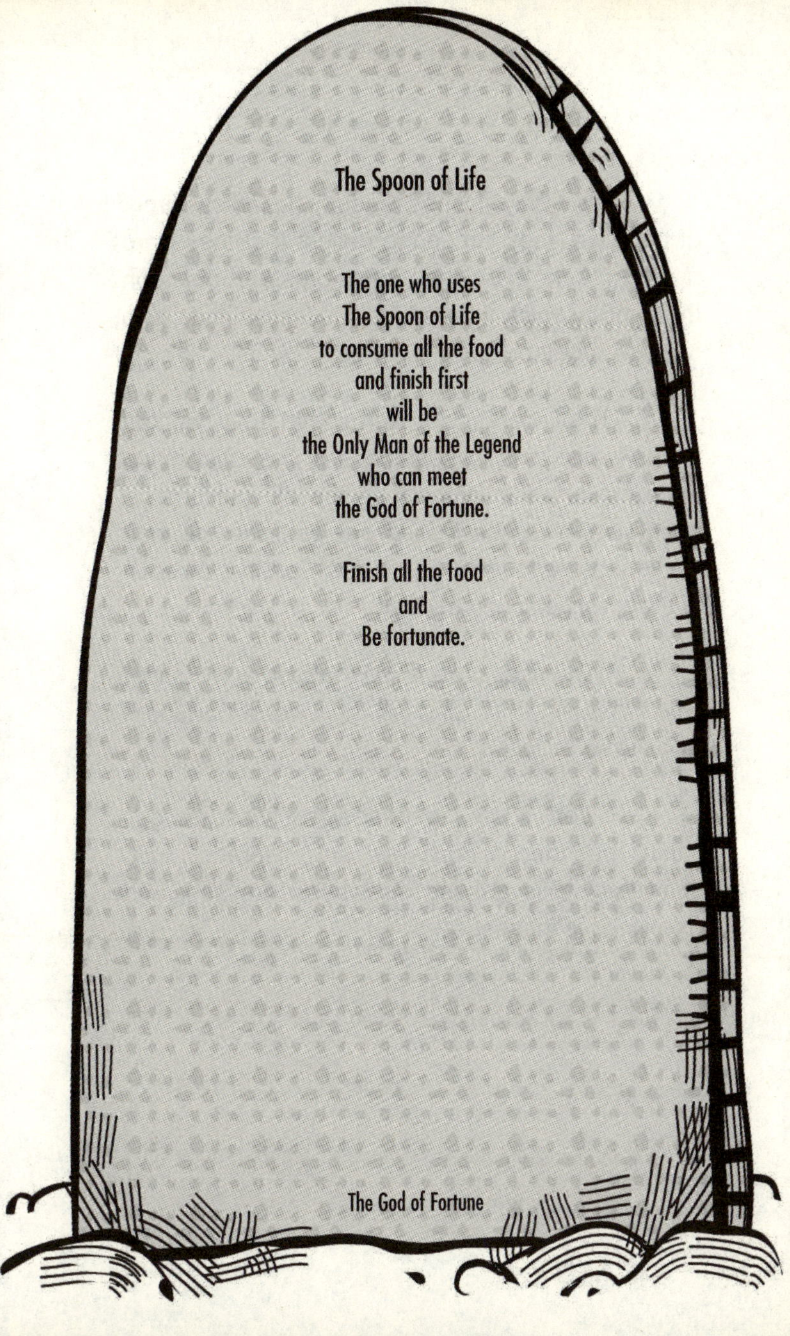
The Spoon of Life
The one who uses
The Spoon of Life
to consume all the food
and finish first
will be
the Only Man of the Legend
who can meet
the God of Fortune.
Finish all the food
and
Be fortunate.
The God of Fortune

After they finished reading the tablet in front of the cave, they jumped in delight that they were right to refuse to pick up the swords and abandon the fight in which they had to kill their friends who traveled together.

They were so cheerful that they wanted to run inside. But the darkness of the cave made them crawl into it instead. All ten did not care to understand why the fastest one to finish the food would be able to meet the God of Fortune, as each of them was starving to death.

“What if all of us finish the food at the same time? Will all ten of us meet the God of Fortune?” Etto asked JoJo.

“I don’t know. I only know that I’m so hungry. I think our friends don’t feel any different,” JoJo answered while groping his way in the dark and following his friends.

They walked until they saw a bright light in front of them. They continued walking as the light became more and more brilliant.

They followed the light until they reached a place that looked like the hall of a palace. In the beautifully decorated white hall, which was furnished with a spectacular chandelier adorned with small pieces of polished glass spheres, a large rectangular dining table was located in the center with chairs made of gold, magnificently reflecting the light of the hall. Artistic paintings were placed all around on the walls.

The table was covered with a white cloth and on this cloth were ten large soup bowls made of gold. Five bowls were placed along both sides of the table, together with ten golden chairs, five chairs positioned on each side. Each chair was as far apart as the distance between the huge soup bowls.

"Oh, it is unbelievable that there is a place like this in a cave. It's more like a palace!" exclaimed Etto.

"I've never seen anything so beautiful and filled with so much gold as this one," said JoJo.

"Let's go and eat because the one who finishes first will have the right to meet the God of Fortune," a man shouted with excitement.

"Let's go. I'm so hungry, I'll eat it all," another man added while running to the dining table.

Everybody rushed to the dining table. Five of them sat on each side, opposite one another, ready to eat the food.

JoJo and Etto sat opposite each other. Everyone happily smiled at one another, although they had not yet seen which kind of food was on the table. They were certain that it was the God of Fortune who magically created these things. But this time it seemed to be special as the food before their eyes was so luxurious and impressive. It was as if they were in a palace full of adornments which ordinary people such as themselves had never touched before.

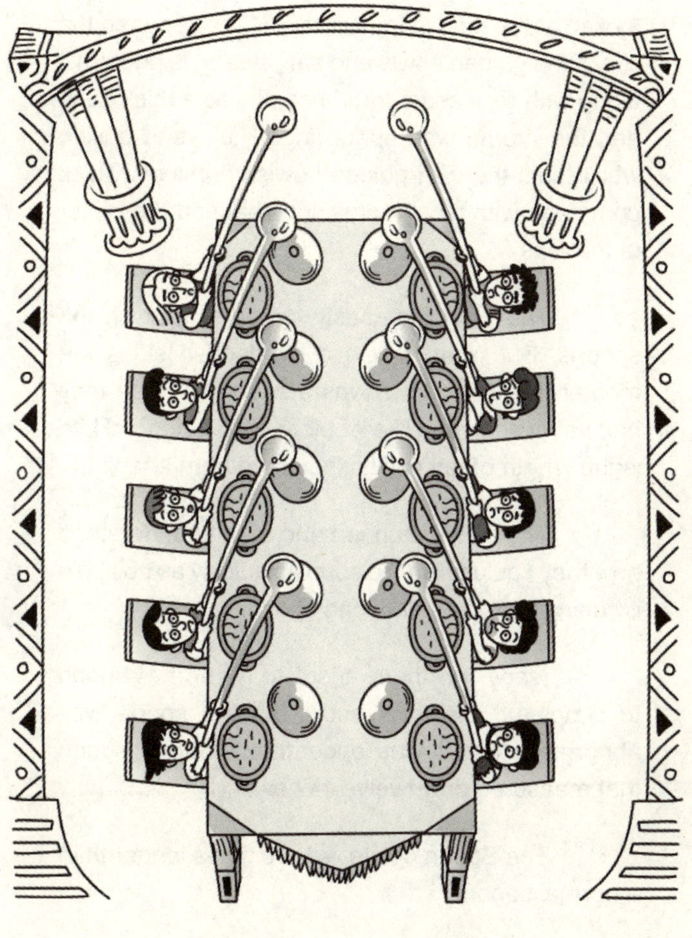

The men were ready in their chairs and looked at the food in front of them. They opened the lids of the golden bowls and saw steam rising from it along with a pleasant fragrance. It was a thick soup and the aroma was appetizing. They read a sign which said the vast golden bowls contained 'Thick corn soup with mushrooms, lobsters and the butter of the Alps'.

They simultaneously turned to pick up the spoons. But what they had overlooked since the moment they sat down was a spoon so large they had never seen one like it before. 'The Spoon of Life is the length of ten cubits' they read from a tablet.

They were stunned and tried to understand how they could finish the soup as quickly as possible by using this weird and long spoon.

Many of them tried to use the spoon to scoop up the thick soup, but the spoon was abnormally long. It was longer than a normal spoon that measured only twelve inches.

The Spoon of Life was 30 times longer than a normal spoon.

The Spoon of Life
The one who uses
The Spoon of Life
to consume all the food
and finish will be
the Only Man of Legend
who can meet
the God of Fortune.
Be fortunate
and
finish all the food.
The God of Fortune

Someone tried to lift the bowl of soup, but he failed because the heavy golden bowl seemed to be fixed to the table. No one could lift it up.

Somebody tried to use the spoon to scoop up the soup, but was unsuccessful because the spoon was extremely long. Some ended up hitting a friend sitting beside them with the hilt of the spoon.

"Why don't you eat?" JoJo asked Etto.

"I've tried to eat but I can't. It's so difficult. What about you? Why haven't you eaten?" Etto replied.

"I want to eat it but I can't. I can see our friends making so many strange gestures. Some look ridiculous," replied JoJo.

"Don't you feel hungry?" asked Etto.

"I do. But I also want to meet the God of Fortune and my desire is no less than any of our friends. Otherwise, I would not risk my life in traveling so far," answered JoJo.

Everybody tried so hard. A considerable amount of time passed and the special thick soup with rare ingredients continued to look hot and appetizing. Unfortunately, no one could even taste a sip of it.

JoJo and Etto made an effort, but they failed too. They could not taste the soup, not even a single drop.

Such a long time passed that some of them started to sweat. Their drops of sweat fell into the soup bowls.

Some of them even cried out of the hunger and suffering they felt because they had food in front of them but couldn't eat it. More significantly, they started to feel hopeless and disappointed by this incident.

The ambience in the hall, which began with laughter, started to change to a stressful atmosphere caused by the collective efforts to eat the food.

Their stress increased with every minute, but no one said a single word.

More and more time passed but no one could gather up any of the soup. Everyone was focused on the problem before them.

Suddenly, a spoon dipped into Etto's bowl and scooped up some of the delicious broth.

Etto looked up and saw that it was the spoon of his beloved friend, Jojo.

"What are you doing, JoJo?" Etto shouted out in anger.

"Trust me...I won't hurt you." JoJo tried to calm his friend down, who became stressful due to his hunger and time-consuming efforts.

JoJo carefully lifted the spoon from Etto's bowl to prevent it from spilling.

"Now, please open your mouth," JoJo said to his friend.

"What are you doing?" Etto questioned.

"I'm going to feed you the soup," replied JoJo.

"Isn't that against the conditions of the God of Fortune?"

"The inscription does not forbid us from feeding each other, it only told us to eat all the food," JoJo explained.

"Now, open your mouth. I'll feed all this soup to you."

Etto opened his mouth and tasted his first sip. He thought it was the most delicious food he had ever tasted in his life. Nothing was as delicious as this soup.

Etto had a second sip and then a third. He continued eating due to the goodwill of JoJo, who fed him more than ten spoons of soup without a single drop hitting the floor.

When he came to the last spoon, Etto stopped and looked at the face of his beloved friend. Then he asked, "Can I feed the soup to you too, my friend? After I have eaten this last spoon, we may never see each other again," Etto said, his voice full of appreciation.

"Thank you so much, Etto," JoJo sincerely thanked his friend.

Etto took his spoon and fed the soup to his friend. JoJo opened his mouth and ate the soup prepared by a god from heaven. JoJo was the second man in the hall who had a chance to eat the specially cooked soup, while their other friends had not yet found a way to taste any.

"It's so tasty. I've never tasted anything so delicious in my life," JoJo said rapturously. The delicious soup instantly made him happy.

"Delicious?" Etto asked with a smile.

"Yes, the most delicious," JoJo replied with a smile too.

"I'll feed you two more spoons," said Etto.

"All right, it's so appetizing." JoJo wanted more of the soup because of his hunger and the pleasant flavor of the food from God.

JoJo had two more spoons of soup. He felt happy and then said to his beloved friend: "That's enough. I'm full already. I'll feed the last spoon to you."

"After this soup is over, we may not see each other again. I would like to thank you, JoJo, for the goodwill you have shown me. Many people come to do business with my family, but all of them are only concerned about their needs. In my life, you are the only one who has done something for me without hoping for anything in return." Etto spoke these words from his heart.

"Don't mention it, we're friends. You should have the last spoon now," JoJo said while holding out the long spoon of soup towards his friend.

Etto had the last spoon of soup fed to him by his beloved friend and then suddenly, a miracle occurred.

A bright white light illuminated the hall and blinded everyone, forcing them to close their eyes. It was like there was a wind circling around each of them, including Etto and JoJo.

They could not open their eyes as everything seemed to be too bright for a person to see.

Soon afterwards, the light was gone together with the wind.

Everybody opened their eyes.

It appeared that they had been transported home.

Everyone was sent home by the magic of the God of Fortune.

"Etto, Etto," a woman called. "Etto, when did you come back, my son?"

It was the voice of Etto's mother calling her son, who had reached home safely.

Etto opened his eyes and saw his mother. He was so glad to see her. She had given him love, warmth and care all his life. He rushed to hug her tightly. He had missed her so much.

"We are all waiting for you. Your father, your siblings and I, we now believe you can do it," Etto's mother said. She had missed him as well.

"Yes, mother. I did it. There were many things that occurred during my adventure over the last few months. I will tell my story to all of you," Etto said excitedly.

The bright white light and the whirlwind brought the entire 1,000,000 home safely. Not one had been injured.

Many people had good memories of the journey. They had made a lot of friends.

The 1,000,000 people had learned plenty of things. They would lead the rest of their lives with the help of the many lessons learned over the past few months. Such lessons they had were called the **Lessons of Life.**

These lessons could not be taught to another person. Everyone has to face issues to get their own true-life experiences.

It is not enough to recount their life's stories to one another. People have to encounter and deal with problems on their own.

LESSONS of LIFE

Many people want to
have a better life than
other people.

Most people just think and dream.

Not many people can
succeed at what they intend to do.

No matter what happens
and whether people succeed or fail,
one thing is for sure,
the people who act will receive the
"Lessons of Life"
or lessons that money cannot buy.

There was only one person who was not taken home. It was JoJo, a young man who became the one in 1,000,000 who experienced the same events as others, but acted in a different way from every other person who set out on the journey.

There was only one person out of a 1,000,000 who was not delivered back to his village and he was the poor orphan boy, JoJo.

The bright white beam also blinded JoJo. He had to shut his eyes tightly. When he opened his eyes again, he found himself in a huge endless sky. He seemed to be in a high place and standing on a large cloud. He could not see where the end of the cloud was.

He surveyed the place. It seemed to him that there was only the sky and this vast cloud, and nothing else.

He wandered farther away from where he first stood but found nothing. He felt strange. It seemed to make him feel warm in his heart and the warmth gradually began to grow.

Suddenly, a strange voice roared. The voice was loud and powerful.

"Hello, young man," said the powerful voice.

JoJo looked around but saw no one. As he turned back to the other side, he saw an old man with a bald head and long, thick eyebrows, which fell down to cover his cheeks. His eyes were bright and filled with warmth. His moustache and beard were around a cubit in length. But his beautiful lips were smiling. A white gown covered his entire body from his head to the tips of his toes.

He held a brown walking stick that had a strange appearance. Its handle was twisted into a circle like the tail of a seahorse.

"Hello, sir," said JoJo.

"Is your name JoJo? How do you feel after passing so many obstacles?" asked the old man.

"Yes, sir. Are you the God of Fortune?" asked JoJo.

"That's right. People call me so," replied the old man.

"Why do you say people always call you so? Aren't you actually the God of Fortune?" JoJo was curious.

"I am merely the one who tests peoples' successes," the old man's answer made the young one more curious.

"Why do others call you the God of Fortune?" Jojo asked

"Why are you here?" the old man questioned in return.

"How do you help people to become fortunate? Do you have magical powers like people say?" Jojo persisted.

JoJo's curiosity had gotten the better of him, that's why he asked so many questions. He wanted answers to the stories he'd heard since he was a child.

"Calm down, I'll tell you the all stories, one by one. Just pay attention," said the old man with a smile.

"I was just an ordinary person like you. When I was a young man, I had dreams. I knew what I wanted and I did everything to pursue them. I overcame many obstructions in my life. I faced as many hardships as you. But as I struggled on, I did well. Finally, I became successful and could fulfill my dreams when I was still young. Later, over the years, I learned from other people. I knew that most people could not make themselves successful. I planned to open an institute in order to teach people. I had a chance to teach a lot of people as I had intended so long, ago. I knew that people wanted to be successful no matter which period they live in. If you were born 20,000 years ago, you may have heard of the **Dreams Come True Institute.** But that was a long time ago and my institute has had successors for many generations."

He continued, "After I died, seven young women who were my students took my place in teaching people. My dream came true and they always supported it by finding more knowledge to educate people. Later, they came to be known as the Seven Angels. They include Mildie, Yumint and their other friends."

"What was your name then?" JoJo asked.

"Jodum, of the Dreams Come True Institute, is my name," the old man answered.

"You've probably never heard of it because it was so long ago. The Seven Angels then ran my institute. The next generation was called the Four Gods of Truth, as people call them."

"Oh, the Seven Angels and the Four Gods of Truth. Will they come here? Will I have a chance to meet them?" JoJo asked.

"Is it heaven or you who chooses the destiny of your life?" asked the old man.

"What do you mean?" JoJo was confused.

"Do you think what you did in life was because heaven assigned it to you or because you chose the destiny of your own life?" the old man asked.

"Honestly, I do not know, sir," replied JoJo.

"Well, I'll tell you a more detailed story," the old man said before he began.

8

Seven Secrets in the Legend of Success

"There are many things people do not know. People always think that they know a lot, and that they are proficient and clever. But finally, they are living beings with a huge brain, which cannot be fully employed and unfortunately, it is abused," the old man told the young man.

JoJo listened intently without interrupting. The old man continued,

"Most people who can work well or have a successful life have to start with the right thoughts and actions, which ultimately amounts to success."

"What people think and do nowadays is contrary to the path to success. With time, fewer people become successful; from one in 10,000 to one in 100,000 and now, it is one in 1,000,000 who makes his life a success. There is one man in every 10,000 years, who can successfully achieve what you and other people seek to do. There are seven secrets, which make people become successful and fortunate. In fact, there is no such thing as fortune. You make your success. No one helps you. Everything is due to the seven right actions only."

"What are the seven secrets? Will I have a chance to know?" JoJo asked with extreme curiosity, obviously showing his excitement. "In fact, you have experienced all seven things already," the old man explained, smiling. "Try to think of all that you confronted since you began your journey. What are those things?"

"If you mean at the beginning, we traveled without knowing our destination. We just walked and followed the North Star, sir," replied JoJo.

"Of course, you have yourself experienced the first secret to success," the old man said and smiled.

"If you recall, many people traveled in order to find me or the God of Fortune. Several million people journeyed to find me. However, only 1,000,000 people chose to follow a star called the North Star. These people started with the right thought. Whenever your thoughts are wrong, you will walk the wrong path, and you will not find the right destination. From millions of people, there remained only 1,000,000 who had the right idea," said the old man.

The First Secret
of
the Legend of Success

is think the right thoughts.

Any person who starts with a wrong idea
will always take the wrong path.

People have to start by finding a map
to navigate their lives.

Most people live by following their instincts.

Animals also live by instincts.
But humans have a brain,
which is many times larger than that of an animal.

Therefore, a successful person
has to depend on his own brain,
exercise his abilities in finding
his own way and not wait for someone to help him.

Most people who fail always
wait for somebody else to help them.
And when they fail, they often blame others.

But failures are caused by their own wrong ideas.

"Can you remember your next obstacle?" asked the old man.

"We came to a huge river with a strong current. We couldn't cross it at first. We had to wait for many months," replied the young man.

"That's right. This is the second secret, which is the obstruction to the path of success. Everybody who wants to succeed will face the same problem. What did you and the other men do?" the old man asked.

"Many people abandoned their journey, but I didn't have a chance to talk to them to find out why. Many of us built small boats, medium-sized boats and large ships. There was also someone who built a raft," answered JoJo.

"The huge river that obstructed your way is like a huge obstacle everyone has to face, whether they were born into a noble family or not." the man explained.

"But there were half of a million people who quit because they thought there was no way they could pass such a huge obstacle."

"People who begin a journey without preparation knowing the potential obstacles or hardships they may confront will have a one in a ten chance to fight or deal with a trying situation."

People who fail always blame obstructions, or the God of Fortune, who did not stand by their side. But they are unaware that there is no such thing in the world as the God of Fortune. Hardships came their way because they built a weak ship, or because of their own mistakes, which they did not concentrate on hard enough. So, unsurprisingly, failure came to them."

The Second Secret
of
the Legend of Success

---

is to do.

Many people who confront obstacles
use the wrong method to cross them.

Many people always quit when
they face problems or obstructions,
whether large or small.

There is one in ten, or merely a 100,000
out of a 1,000,000 people, who act right.

Nine out of ten people often think that
what they do is right.

They are careless and they underestimate obstructions.

They do not prepare themselves
for a lot of obstacles, which are ready
to attack their lives like storms,
or waves that come
with the eagerness to ruin everything.

Only one out of ten
is well prepared for bad situations.
He does not wait for support
from anybody, or any help from any god.

"What was the next thing you confronted?" asked the old man.

"From the remaining 100,000 from that entered the land of ogres, screams of fear were heard. I felt afraid," the young man answered.

"There were only 10,000 out of a 100,000 who left that land. Each of us told stories about the ogres they had met. None of the ogres we spoke about looked alike. Some said that their ogre had three heads. Others said that it had ten arms. A few were sure it had a green body or that it carried a club with spikes on it."

The old man began to laugh. He said, "You passed it all. I'd like to tell you a story to make you understand, since you are the only person of the legend who could overcome all the obstacles. You need to know the truth, so that you can tell many people and make them understand, too."

The Third Secret
of
the Legend of Success

---

is the Power of the Subconscious.

People have collected so many stories,
thoughts and knowledge
and now, these have become part of
the thinking process in their brains.

People who think, act and speak well,
as well as create good things, will find only good stories in life.

People who think wickedly will collect
these feeling in their brains.
Thus, evil thoughts will occur.

Monsters of the imagination do not exist.

But what people see is caused by
their own creation without them being aware of it.
It is due to the collection of bad ideas.

The more people think about bad issues,
the more they find their monster of imagination dreadful.

Therefore, this tells us that there is
only one in ten men who thinks, speaks and does well.

Hence, his life becomes successful.

"And what was your next encounter?" The old man asked.

"We walked through a desert. Some of us dropped to the ground during the journey. Some didn't have enough food. Some gave up because they lost their strength, while others saw mirages in the desert. Not many people were left when we exited the desert; there were only 1,000 out of 10,000," JoJo replied.

"This is about planning, preparation and making our body and mind ready to confront the many challenges in life. It's because our life is not as easy as we think. So, there remained only one out of ten people, which is so sad," said the old man.

The Fourth Secret
of
the Legend of Success

---

is planning for the future.

Life is a journey and during this journey we will find
unexpected events.

Many situations
we confront are unpredictable.

A lot of people have their dreams
and everything is beautiful to them.

This is not strange for
positive-minded people,
since they will see everything in a pleasant way.

This is caused by a good subconscious.
However, what we cannot lack is good planning.

Issues in life will not become bad
if we learn good planning, carefulness
and knowledge about the optimum use of our resources.

Only one in ten
has a good plan for his life.

"After there remained only 1,000 men, what was the next obstruction you found?" the old man asked.

"We found ten caves. Each cave had a sign stating its name. We divided ourselves into ten groups. Each group consisted of 100 people."

"Can you remember which caves there were?" asked the old man.

"Yes sir, they were:

Cave of Money
Cave of Gold
Cave of Power
Cave of Treasures
Cave of Blessedness
Cave of Family
Cave of Health
Cave of Wealth
Cave of Work
Cave of Happiness."

"You chose the Cave of Work, didn't you? Everyone has the right to choose their own path and you've chosen it. The fact that you can stand here is not because I chose you, but because you chose it yourself," said the man smiling.

The Fifth Secret
of
the Legend of Success

---

is the Choices of Life.

There are a lot of choices in everyone's life.

Most people, if they have a chance,
will choose comfort as their priority.

Another group of people will choose
happiness or something else that
brings more happiness to their lives.

We always get what we've chosen.
But only one in ten choose work.

Working brings us hardships,
before it gives us comfort in the end.

The men who are diligent,
work cleverly and always find
more knowledge will achieve stable
and sustainable comfort
in the final stage of their lives.

"Many people choose what they want and they really get it. But something like that is merely temporary happiness, a physical object. When they die, they cannot take money with them. Everything depends on our decisions. People who are disappointed, think evil or feel jealous of others and will blame the God of Fortune for not taking their side. This is because people who choose money or gold get these things easily, but do not know how to keep it. They don't know how to save and how to make a fortune from money and gold. In contrast, they spend it extravagantly. They gamble and use it unwisely, which will cause trouble later. Perhaps this can be defined as being comfortable at the beginning and suffering at the end. Hardships at the end of your life are the result of a lack of the right principles of working. Then, this can cause failure to anyone's life," said the old man, giving a detailed clarification.

"What did you find next?" he then asked.

"Swords, sir. There were 90 swords for the remaining 100 men who chose the path of Work."

"You didn't grab a sword, did you?"

"No, I didn't, sir. I was among the ten people who did not pick up a sword," JoJo replied to the old man.

"Why didn't you take a sword?" asked the old man.

"I didn't want to kill anyone in order to be a special person or become superior by killing others," JoJo answered.

"Young man, I wonder if you realize that you are among the few men who have stood in this position. It's true that there might be only ten out of a 100 men, because the rest disappeared on the way. I think that most people want power, money, blessedness or gold, and what they always do is kill their fellow men to get it," the old man went on.

"There may be only ten out of 1,000,000 men who think like this. This is a part of success blended with happiness."

"What does 'blended with happiness' mean, sir?" JoJo asked.

The old man explained, "The one who wins by killing others might become as successful as they desire, but this needs cruelty. This type of successful person has a rough mind and lacks happiness, although he gets all the physical objects he desires."

The Sixth Secret
of
the Legend of Success

---

is to conquer one's own mind.

The ultimate winner does not
beat other people all the time,
as there are many people in the world
and proficient people are countless.

The true ultimate winner
wins one's own mind without
thinking about harming other people.

Everybody who wants success in life has the same needs,
but each applies different methods.

Most people step on others' heads to move higher.

Most people choose to hurt others to become superior.

Most people choose to betray friends and bosses for their own benefit,
without caring about the troubles of other people.

There are only ten out of 1,000,000
who do not think about jostling by using such sinful methods.

Hence, only a few people
become successful in life.

"Then, what was the last impediment you confronted?" the old man asked the boy.

"I did not think it was an obstruction, sir," said JoJo.

"So, what did you think it was?" the old man questioned.

"There were ten of us that entered the cave which looked like a palace. Inside, it was beautifully furnished and ornately decorated. Everything was made of gold," JoJo retold the story.

"What else did you find?" the old man probed.

"A long golden spoon that no one could scoop up the soup with. I couldn't do it either," replied JoJo.

"Well, what did you do?" asked the old man.

"I fed the soup to my friend until he finished his bowl and then I came here. I feel a little confused because my friend, Etto, was the first one who finished the soup because I fed it to him. I only had a few sips of the soup," JoJo replied.

“Your generosity is hard to find. At that time, no one would have done what you did. Other people who were watching you might have thought you were stupid,” the old man continued.

Sometimes, stupidity and goodness are so close that we cannot differentiate between the two. Most people would think that such behavior is stupid, because what you did would not bring you any benefit, but it was done for another person.

“How do we know whether what we do is stupid or good, sir?” JoJo asked curiously.

“You’ve asked a very good question. A good person always does things for the public’s benefit. When he sees that other people are happy, he also feels happy. That is the trait of a good person.

A person who is only concerned about his own welfare will always think how much he will gain first. He is selfish and may pretend that he does something for others, but actually, he is solely thinking about his own good. Such a person is regarded as bad and foolish.”

The Seventh Secret
of
the Legend of Success

is to do good things.
The more time passes,
the more people long for their own benefits and happiness.

Jostling and hatred seems to be normal for people.

People who forget goodness
will not become truly successful,
since true success must contain
HAPPINESS in it.

If the world lacks giving, sharing,
kindness and generosity,
this world will become dull and lack happiness.

It will turn into a world where people harm,
blame, accuse and kill each other.

Only one in 1,000,000
is kind and generous.

Such a person would do anything for others
without hoping for something in return.

"Young man, do you know that the hardships you confronted are the tests you have already passed?" the old man continued. "You are the one in 1,000,000 or the one in 10,000 years who can come here to talk to me. What happened to you was not luck. It was not destiny from heaven and no one assigned it to you. The truth is that people who fail and have a sinful mind will blame their failure on everything that made them feel disappointed. They blame everything that made them fail.

It is not so hard to make yourself successful. The Secrets of the Legend of Success are not so complex, are they?

The things you did made you superior to others. These seven principles are simple and practical. Everybody can practise them.

I hope you will follow your dreams and become as successful as you wish by applying these seven rules to your daily life. Soon, you will find happiness and success.

Do you have any more questions?" the old man inquired finally.

"Yes, I do, sir. Does this mean that there is no God of Fortune in this world?" asked JoJo.

"No, such a god is simply a part of the imagination of losers. The fact is simple: People who fail and do not understand or follow the seven principles always think that they are unlucky and the God of Fortune does not take their side. It is just a disparaging story people make up. They do not look to see how they can succeed. They just blame anything they can and that a life more favorable to them is something that does not exist. They simply want to be lazy about their failures," the old man explained.

"Will I have a chance to meet you again, sir?" JoJo asked.

"If you live another 10,000 years, maybe you will meet me again," answered the old man with a twinkle in his eye.

"What if I confront obstructions while working? What should I do, sir?" JoJo asked.

"I will ask the seven angels to help people while I am away for meditation. You should find your way to meet them. Then, they will teach you how to improve your work," the old man advised.

"You have to be confident in yourself and your abilities, as well as be faithful to yourself. Now you know everything that will lead you to the path of success," said the old man.

Jojo was filled with faith in himself and had gained immense knowledge through his past experiences. This made him feel energetic to fight and hope for success. More importantly, he knew the secrets that others did not know yet.

JoJo memorized everything that happened, including the conversation with the old man, Professor Jodum of the Dreams Come True Institute, who taught many people to become successful for the past 20,000 years. This enabled the young man to learn about experiences of successful people within a short span of time.

And now, he was ready to fight the obstacles that would happen in the remainder of his life. He was ready to tell these stories to his friends, relatives and people in the village who wanted to know how to walk the path to success in detail.

The young man fell to his knees and paid respect to the old man with all his heart. Then he said, “Thank you very much, Professor Jodum.”

“I wish you luck,” the professor replied.

Suddenly, a brilliant white light flashed and then Professor Jodum disappeared.

JoJo had suddenly returned to his village, where he’d begun his journey.

He thought to himself how he would definitely do everything Professor Jodum had taught him. More significantly, he was ready to share and tell his story of success to everyone he knew in his own words.

"Thank you, Professor," he shouted at the top of his lungs as he ran into his house with extreme joy.

Do everything
confidently
and constantly,
without changing.

Do not
be afraid of
doing good deeds.

But
be ashamed of
hurting others,

both
physically
and mentally.

For any person
who does
good things
without hoping
for rewards,
that person will
become a
fortunate man.

DAMRONG PINKOON was born in Bangkok, Thailand, in November1972. He graduated with a Bachelor's Degree in Business Administration and a Marketing Major from The University of Thai Chamber of Commerce, Bangkok, Thailand (UTCC). He also attended the College of Management of Mahidol University (CMMU) from where he graduated with a Master's Degree in Management.

DAMRONG PINKOON started working with Thai Carbon Black Public Company Limited (Birla Group from India) and then moved to Thai Escorp Limited, a Japanese company based in Bangkok, Thailand with its headquarters in Shinsho Corporation in Tokyo, Japan.

DAMRONG PINKOON started his own business in Bangkok in 1999 called "Rester Massage Chair" when he was 26 years old. He was a successful business man and his business became talk of the town within four years and today is one of the most successful businesses in the luxury seating sector.

After tasting success in business, he began writing many pocket books which became bestsellers in his hometown. As a well-known author, he was invited to speak at seminars, advised other corporations and individuals and became an instructor of business strategies.

His philosophy books and how-to novels have been translated into many languages in the past few years and have since gone on to be bestsellers on the international book scene.

Damrong Pinkoon

Special Thanks

Ms. Sirisara Pinkoon	for all the support
Ms. Daranee Rattanathum	for assisting and corr
Ms. Chompoo Trakullersathien	for translation
Mr. Philip Hall	for editing
Ms. Uchenee Puttichard	for assisting

And thanks again for everything
I've learned from all my professors.
And to the great writers who wrote great books,
thank you for making it all possible for me.